Fis

NICHOLAS WISEMAN

Nicholas Wiseman was born in 1802 in Seville where his father was a merchant. Both sides of his family had their roots in Ireland. While an infant his mother consecrated him to the service of the Church in Seville Cathedral. After his father's early death his mother returned to Ireland, but she sent him at the age of eight to board in England at Ushaw College in Co. Durham. Here he was treated with favour by Dr. Lingard, the Vice Rector, who was already researching for his magisterial *History of England*.

At the age of sixteen he was one of the small party of students sent to Rome to study at the Venerable English College after its restoration by Pius VII. He gained his Doctorate after the usual public disputation, and because of his high linguistic and scholastic abilities won an open competition for the post of Professor of Oriental Languages at the University of Rome. He was frequently received by Pius VII, and at the age of 26 was appointed Rector of the English College. His hugely popular lectures in London in 1835 and 1836 on the Catholic Faith, given largely to Protestant audiences, brought him national fame. In 1850 he was made a Cardinal and chosen by Pius IX to restore the ecclesiastical hierarchy in England. When he took up office Catholics were still largely a persecuted sect; by the time of his death in 1865 they had come to be accepted as members of a Church which was playing an increasingly significant role in national life.

Despite his episcopal duties Cardinal Wiseman continued to pursue his scholarly and artistic interests. In 1854 he published a successful novel, *Fabiola*, about early Christians in Rome, and in 1858 his *Recollections of the Last Four Popes and of Rome in their Times*.

Published by Fisher Press, Post Office Box 41,
Sevenoaks, Kent TN15 6YN, England

The text of *Leo XII and Pius VIII* was first published in 1858
as part of
Nicholas Wiseman's
*Recollections of the Last Four Popes
and of Rome in their Times*

First published as a Fisher paperback 2005

British Library Cataloguing in Publication Data

A catalogue record for this book is available from
The British Library

ISBN 1 874037 18 3

Printed by Antony Rowe (Eastbourne) Ltd

NICHOLAS WISEMAN

LEO
THE TWELTH

Fisher Press

ACKNOWLEDGEMENTS

We are grateful to the Reverend Richard Whinder for his encouragement in the production of this volume and for much help in elucidating some of the biographical and historical background to Cardinal Wiseman's accounts.

INTRODUCTION

NICHOLAS Wiseman published his recollections of Leo XII and Pius VIII in 1858. It was eight years since he had been the papal choice to restore the English hierarchy and nearly thirty years since their reigns had ended.[1]

They had ruled in succession for little more than seven years in the eighteen-twenties. Their policies were frequently, indeed usually, misunderstood at the time, particularly by those with a simplistic notion that material progress and democratic institutions were the sole source of human happiness. Their true worth and significance were often only fully understood much later, by those with a greater perception of eternal truths.

Leo XII had had misgivings about the general decline of moral standards and religious observance in the Papal States and abroad long before he became pope. Later, as a sovereign territorial ruler, and the spiritual head of the Catholic Church, he had both the legal power, and, as he saw it, the moral duty to introduce measures to help restore what had been lost, repudiated or forgotten.

In 1825 he proclaimed a papal Jubilee, the first for fifty years. To the surprise of many there was a great outpouring of religious fervour among the thousands of pilgrims who flocked to Rome. A perceptive observer might have seen in this response a sign that public sentiment was subconsciously preparing for the great Catholic revival and expansion which occured later in the century. Yet his ministers and the cardinals in Rome had been largely opposed to the celebrations. They were concerned about the security implications of large crowds gathering in what were beginning to be turbulent times.

1. Wiseman's reflections on the life and times of the previous pope are contained in *Pius VII* (Fisher Press, 2003).

Most European governments were also hostile. However, as Wiseman records, some members of the ruling dynasties of Europe could not resist coming themselves to Rome, albeit in disguise, and sharing the three days of simple fare in the pilgrims' hostels which the Pope provided for all.

Catholic Emancipation was finally granted in England in 1829. By 1858, when Wiseman was publishing his account, it was clear that, with the removal of restrictions, Catholics were now playing an increased part in national life. There had also been an impact on potential converts, previously perhaps sensitive to the legal disadvantages that a change of religious allegiance would have involved before the Act.

Leo XII reigned from 28 September 1823 till his death on 19 February 1829. Wiseman's personal indebtedness to him was profound. It was Leo's introduction of open competition for university posts in the Papal States that had enabled Wiseman to obtain the chair of Oriental Languages at the Roman University at the astonishingly early age of twenty-four. And it is likely that the Pope's personal encouragement and support put the young Wiseman on the path that led from the rectorship of the Venerable English College in Rome to the highest office of the Church in England.

Leo's successor, Pius VIII, reigned for just twenty months, from 31 March 1829 to 1 December 1830. Wiseman speaks of his deep personal devotion to him. He recalls that it was during his brief pontificate that Catholic Emancipation was finally achieved. The celebrations which the students held at the English College in Rome to mark this momentous event, lovingly described by Wiseman, were quintessentially English. It was also Pius VIII who appointed Thomas Weld, a member of a prominent Catholic recusant family, as the first English Cardinal since the Reformation.

Wiseman's recollections incorporate vivid human sketches and anecdotes when he describes and assesses the major political and religious events of the two reigns. It was an important time of transition. After the defeat of

Napoleon in 1815, Pius VII's Secretary of State, Cardinal Consalvi, had reestablished effective administration in the Papal States, now once more under the Pope's rule. Yet, as Leo XII had observed, less had been done to raise the moral and spiritual condition of its citizens, or to make a specifically Catholic impact on the outside world. Consalvi, the consummate statesman who had triumphed at the Congress of Vienna which followed Napoleon's defeat, was worn-out by the time of the conclave that elected Leo XII. However, most cardinal electors and many prominent thinkers in Europe were also by now coming to the view that a thorough restoration of moral and religious values was needed.

In his *Saints and Sinners: A History of the Popes*, Eamon Duffy perceptibly summarizes the climate of opinion prevailing before Leo XII's accession.

Catholicism in the Age of Enlightenment had no place in its heart for the Papacy. The Pope's spiritual authority was acknowledged but minimised, and it was imagined in juridical or administrative terms. It belonged to the ordering of Church, not to the essence of the faith. Reform-minded Catholics saw nothing wrong in the prince or the state placing restrictions on the interference of popes.[1]

Duffy explains that the French Revolution and the Terror that followed, and Napoleon's efforts to turn the Church and the Popes into aspects of Imperial policy, changed this perception. The new requirement was most succinctly expressed by Count Joseph de Maistre, the Sardinian Ambassador to St Petersburg in his treatise *Du Pape* of 1819:

There can be no public morality and no national character without religion; there can be no Christianity without Catholicism; there can be no Catholicism without the Pope; there can

1. Duffy, *Saints and Sinners—A History of the Popes*, Yale Book, 2002, p. 275.

be no Pope without the sovereignty that belongs to him.

Duffy expands on this. "As the century unfolded, the exaltation of the papacy at the heart of Catholicism, 'Ultramontanism' as it was called, would increasingly dominate Catholic thinking.[1]

Although his historical analysis of the intellectual climate in the years leading up to Leo XII's accession is perceptive, he appears not to have studied in depth the encyclicals and decrees of his reign, and completely ignores Leo's aims and successes. Indeed, Duffy's sketchy comments contrast with his own detailed work in his magisterial *Voices of Morebath*. Duffy presents himself here not as an unbiased historian of the reign but as a propagandist for liberal Catholicism.

That is why it is so important that we have the balanced recollections of Wiseman. He actually knew Leo, lived and worked in Rome throughout his pontificate, saw him on a regular basis, and had close relations with all who worked with him.

Duffy sets the critical tone in the following way.

"...Annibale della Genga (Leo XII), a sickly sixty-three year old, crippled by chronic haemorrhoids, disapproved of Pius VII's and Consalvi's policies and wanted a stronger, more conservative regime in papal territory... Leo was a contrast with Consalvi in every way. Pious, puritanical (though he shocked the cardinals by his passion for shooting birds in the Vatican gardens) and confrontational, he lacked political realism."[2]

1. Ibid. p. 276.
2. Ibid. p. 278. The contrast drawn by Duffy between Leo XII and Cardinal Consalvi is overstated. Wiseman's account of the life and achievements of the Cardinal in his recollections of Pius VII seems more balanced, as is his understanding of Pope Leo. Consalvi, although remaining in deacon's orders, was by no means unpious; the high favour in which he was held by the saintly Pius VII would have precluded this.

As the first example of Leo's "lack of political realism" Duffy cites his decision to reinstate the annual tribute from the Kingdom of Naples of a palfrey, a saddle horse. Duffy praises Consalvi who, as Secretary of State of Pius VII, had earlier commuted this entirely to a cash payment. Duffy's view is that this ancient form of tribute was a sore point as it reminded the Neapolitans or the Government of Naples (Duffy does not specify to which he refers) of its ancient feudal dependency on Rome. However, it is arguable that the restoration of the old custom better symbolised the revival of the longstanding traditional friendship between Naples and the Papal States after an extended period in the eighteenth century in which the Government of the Two Sicilies (which included the Kingdom of Naples) was anti-clerical and under the strong influence of Freemasonry. It is by no means certain that "modernising" the tribute of a pal-frey, by changing it to a cash payment, raised by taxing the Neapolitan clergy, was not also open to criticism.

In his *The History of the Papacy in the XIXth Century*, the Danish historian, Frederik Nielsen, a Protestant with little sympathy for Leo's internal religious and social measures, praises the effectiveness of Leo's diplomatic relations with foreign powers, describing them as "very successful."[1] Leo consolidated links with the France of

He was confrontational when this was required: an example of his defiance was his public refusal to recognise Napoleon I's divorce from the Empress Josephine and subsequent remarriage to Marie-Louise of Austria. As a prelate Consalvi had to mix in diplomatic circles in which there were those who lived at variance from the teachings of the Church. But there is nothing to suggest that he was himself lax in his personal behaviour. Leo XII certainly had high moral standards and was deeply religious. Yet although abstemious in his private life he did not stint himself in performing the colourful traditional church ceremonies which had often been delegated to others by his predecessor. Wiseman's detailed picture of Leo makes abundantly apparent that "puritanical" is quite indequate as a summary of this pope's complex character.
1. pp. 26-27. London, 1906.

Charles X. On pastoral grounds, he provided new bishops for the long vacant dioceses of the countries of South America, despite the opposition of the conservative Spanish Government which still claimed sovereignty over, and wished to influence appointments in, these now independent former colonies. He also reached a satisfactory Concordat with the Government of the Netherlands to protect Catholics in Belgium. And he used his contacts with prominent political figures in England to promote the cause of Catholic Emancipation which was finally achieved soon after his death.

Both Nielsen and Duffy, however, regard Leo's internal policies as both unrealistic and undesirable. The Pope was undoubtedly ready to risk considerable personal unpopularity to do what he believed to be right.

In his first encyclical, "*Ubi primum*" he showed his determination to raise the clergy's intellectual, moral and disciplinary standards. He followed this up with a programme of reducing the huge disparities of income among the clergy of the parishes in Rome. This egalitarian measure was not "conservative" if by this is meant preserving the *status quo* or favouring better-off priests.

A purge of inefficient or venal curial officials followed. Those accustomed to taking long unauthorised holidays during the whole of the Roman summer were surprised to find on their return that their places had been taken by others. The explanation they received was that their unauthorised absences had been taken as a sign that they wished to give up their offices!

Leo had difficulties too with the College of Cardinals because of his determination to enforce economies and root out abuses. Yet, although determined to reduce unnecessary public expenditure, one of his early acts was to lower several taxes on the citizens of the Papal States. He also reduced legal fees and expenses so as to make justice cheaper for his subjects, with the less well-off benefiting most from the measure.

By 1825, through the efforts of his Treasurer-General, Belisario Cristaldi, he was able to reduce land taxes throughout the Papal States by a massive 25 per cent. Wiseman indicates that this gave a huge boost to industry.

Public finances remained healthy throughout the rest of the reign. The expenses of the Jubilee were adequately covered, including the three days board and lodging for all pilgrims. Sums were even able to be put aside for a measure, dear to Leo's heart, to repurchase the immense landed property in the Papal States that had been settled on Prince Eugene Napoleon and his heirs before the restoration of Papal rule. The estates were badly administered by absentee landlords and a cause for local resentment. By the time of his death Leo had almost succeeded in assembling the funds to buy the family out.

Pope Leo's personal life was one of the strictest economy, with his own expenses costing no more than a *scudo* a day. Chateaubriand, the former French Foreign Minister and at that time French Ambassador to his Court, describes an audience with him in the autumn of 1828 as follows:

Sa Sainteté me reçut en audience privée; les audiences publiques ne sont pas de usage et coûtent trop cher. Leo XII, prince d'une grand taille et d'un air à la fois serein et triste, est vêtu d'une simple soutane blanche; il n'a aucun faste et se tient dans un cabinet pauvre, presque sans meubles. Il ne mange presque pas; il vit, avec son chat,[1] d'un peu de polenta.[2]

But his personal austerity did not mean that he stinted

1. Chateaubriand adopted Leo's cat after the Pope's death.
2. [His Holiness received me in a private audience. Public audiences are no longer usual and cost too much. Leo XII, a very tall Prince, had an air at once serene and sad. He was dressed in a simple white soutane. He kept no state and we sat in a simple study with almost no furniture. He hardly eats anything. He lives, with his cat, on a little polenta.]

spending money where he believed it essential or appropriate. He allocated huge funds for the rebuilding of San
Paulo's Cathedral outside the Walls which had been
almost completely destroyed by fire as his predecessor lay
dying. He added the Baptistery to Santa Maria Maggiore,
instituted public works to protect the citizens of Tivoli
from flooding of the river Anio, authorised expenditure on
the excavations of the Etruscan sites in Tuscany, and set in
hand the creation of an Etruscan Museum in the Vatican.
Yet, as Wiseman makes clear, he was personally opposed to
having his own name recorded on those monuments,
buildings or public works which had been initiated by him
during his reign.

What many liberals in politics and religion, both then
and now, have found most difficult to accept was the Pope's
decision to take energetic action on law and order, to
encourage more committed religious observance, to protect
family life, and to support traditional morality.

He instituted a highly successful campaign to eradicate
brigands who controlled large parts of the Appenine
mountains and ran protection rackets over wide areas.
Wiseman records from his early days in Rome the pathetic
sight of savagely mutilated beggars who were known to
have informed the authorities about the brigands' criminal rackets and extortion, or who had sought to stand up
to them.

Under Leo XII's new decree, bandits could be summarily
executed within twenty-four hours of their arrest. In practice those who showed adequate signs of repentance were
often reprieved, given gaol sentences, or sent into exile.
By his other economic measures the Pope hoped to raise
the conditions of the poorest in the countryside so that
they would be able to give up brigandage or resist it in
their villages.

It was an age of secret societies, including Freemasonry
and the revolutionary Carbonari. The Pope was particularly concerned about their influence in universities. On 13

March 1825 he issued a Bull proscribing Freemasonry. This reiterated the earlier papal condemnations of Clement XII and Pius VII. Other secret societies were also proscribed. On 31 August Cardinal Ravoralla pronounced sentence on more than 500 persons of all ages and occupations. A very few were condemned to death (there had been a plot against the life of the Pope), some were imprisoned (in far from harsh conditions). But the vast majority were allowed their liberty under the supervision of the police. Ravoralla, in an attempt to bring some of the dissidents round to a more stable life, provided dowries to women who might make them suitable wives!

On the social front the Pope introduced a series of measures to support family life. Italian bars were forbidden to sell alcoholic drinks for consumption within their premises; they had to be purchased from grills opening on to the street. This was to discourage men from spending long hours in public bars which the Pope believed had led to drunkeness and often violent brawls. Its objective was to enourage drinkers to take their alcohol home to consume with their families. It was not, as can be imagined, a popular measure, and some said that it simply encouraged more drunkeness in the street. Wiseman's view was that it might well have been successful in its objective if it had received a longer trial. But the measure was widely unpopular and repealed at the beginning of the reign of Pius VIII.

Gambling, a cause of debt for many, was discouraged by laws forbidding games on Sundays and feast days. In a further attempt to restrict over-borrowing, often used for gambling purposes, or to repay the resulting debts, business transactions were forbidden between Christians and Jews.

Jewish money-lenders were a major source of borrowing and hence seen as a contributing factor in citizens' problems of indebtedness. The Pope has been subsequently much criticised for this, and for other measures taken against the Jews. They were once more required to live in the Ghetto, although public land was provided to make this larger, and the district was provided with a new internal fountain and water supply. Mindful of the Christian duty to convert the Jews, laws were also passed to require leading Jews in Rome to attend Christian services regularly. It is sometimes argued by church leaders today that the requirements of ecumenism mean that the Christian duty to bring others to Christ is no longer appropriate. Leo XII took a different view. It is worth recording that a number of those received into the Church during the Jubilee of 1825 were Jews.

There was also a measure intended to discourage some public behaviour which had become gross in the eyes of many: women were forbidden to wear tight-fitting dresses, and a group of ancient statues offensive to Christian modesty which were displayed in a gallery created by his predecessor were removed. Leo personally purchased the plates of some engravings of Canova and had them destroyed as inconsistent with moral delicacy.

In the years after the end of the Napoleonic conflict there was a huge increase in the number of visitors who flocked to Rome as the climax of the Grand Tour. Many came just to visit its churches for their architecture and the art that they contained, or for their beautiful liturgies. Some tourists were notably disrespectful of the piety of others. Both popes came to doubt whether the earlier spirit of tolerance and indulgence was in the moral and spiritual interests either of their subjects, or of the visitors themselves. Measures were therefore taken to discourage irreverent behaviour in churches, particularly during services. Some elements of this requirement for modesty of dress in churches remain to this day in the Vatican State.

In his account of his management of internal affairs Duffy ignores the fact that Leo was the ruler of a state and thus responsible for setting the tone of public morality. He completely ignores Pope Leo's great Jubilee of 1825, the single most important event of his pontificate, and of major importance for the world-wide Church. What is interesting is that within a few years of these "illiberal" measures public

morality and religious commitment in many parts of Europe
at all levels of society did begin to show the first signs of
impovement—it was not only Queen Victoria who had higher moral standards than her parents! In the decades that
followed there was also a significant growth in church attendance and religious practice, and a prolonged new era of new
church building began. Clearly there were complex factors at
work in this process of change. But there is no doubt that
the popes' actions in the eighteen-twenties sent out a powerful signal of moral and religious leadership to the world that
the standards of European societies were too low, and that
they could, and should, be raised.

The adoption of a new saint during a papal reign often
provides an important indication both of the spirit of the
times, and of the preoccupations of the Holy Father and his
advisers when the cause for canonisation is being promoted.
It is significant that it was during Leo XII's papacy that Peter
Damian, the austere 11th century Camaldolese Benedictine
monk, was canonised. As a commited reformer, St Peter had
preached and written against the marriage of the clergy, laxi-
ty within monastic orders, and simony; and he also took an
active part in helping to promote regular canonical life for
cathedral clergy, and in the reform of the papacy.

From a Christian point of view there are issues here for
consideration in our own times. The moral standards in
much of today's developed world are probably as bad if not
worse than those in Europe before the 1820s. Crime and
threats to security from groups hostile to the established
order and its traditions are similarly of concern. Radical
Islam attacks the moral standards of the West. The philosophic conflicts which raged in the early years of the
nineteenth century are still with us. Many today regard the
"Age of Enlightenment" as the true beginning of the modern world, and hence something to be welcomed
unreservedly. They see its teaching of reliance on reason
alone as the only sound basis for modern human endeavour.

On the other side are those who not only accept divine

revelation as true, but have come to see it as the most ratio-
nal explanation of the nature of man and of the universe,
and hence the basis for true morality. The rejection of any
place for God in the European Constitution, and the recent
blocking by the European Parliament of the appointment of
a Catholic with orthodox views on religion and morality as
a European Commissioner, show the way the wind is currently blowing on the continent as a whole.

In Britain the hostility shown by the BBC towards
Catholics and Catholic teaching on issues of sexual morality, the right to life of the baby in its mother's womb, and
the propaganda put out constantly in favour of euthanasia,
is well documented. The BBC combines this with a readiness to caricature and ridicule the teachings of the Church.
This is done by selective interviewing, commissioning pro-
grammes that highlight the Church's failures wherever they
occur, or which ridicule the Church and the Pope; and by
giving regular air time to those hostile to the Church, or to
those who, while continuing to proclaim their Church
membership, dissent from its fundamental teachings.

In Parliament and the higher echelons of the Civil
Service there are many who wish to make it impossible
for those with orthodox Catholic views to teach in
schools, practise medicine, or work in the Health Service,
without either concealing or repudiating their beliefs, or
facing the prospect of being marginalised. It is already
very difficult for an orthodox Catholic to pass successfully
an interview for admission to the Civil Service or local
government, if certain topics come up in discussion and
the candidate speaks freely.

What can be done? The first step is clearly to mobilise
opinion for a restoration of traditional moral and religious
values, and, where possible, to change the law to encourage
and support this restoration. Perhaps the will to do this is currently more widespread in the United States than in Europe.

Anyone seeking to promote initiatives to support the traditional family and encourage citizens in the pursuit of the

traditional Christian standards of behaviour and religious practice, should find it of value to consider how these issues were tackled in the past by a papal Government with these avowed aims. Despite the obvious differences between the moral and political climate in the second decade of the nineteenth century and the first decade of the twenty-first, the practical steps which these two popes took to tackle their concerns are worth examining critically and the possibilities evaluated.

And if we in Europe are not yet at the point where a regime change might give some hope of reforming action, there is at least scope for an honest assessment of the consequences of the liberal attitudes and policies that have been pursued by European states and have contributed to the moral and religious disintegration that currently faces us.

The tragedy is that the intentions of liberal reformers, many of whom were men of compassion and of integrity, seemed so laudable—they were seeking to create a tolerant and fairer society; they looked back with regret and disapproval on what they saw as the authoritarianism and repression of past governments, or of religious institutions.

But the actual results of the measures and schemes introduced to bring about changes that they expected to be for the better were often, however, quite different from what the originators intended. The philosophic assumption behind much of their programme was that human beings would behave in a responsible and moral way if only they were trusted with extensive political and moral freedom, and coercion was removed.

History seems to teach, however, that without either a strong moral code ingrained in the vast majority of citizens, or a powerful government committed to protecting the weak, the government of a state or locality can quite easily become a victim of powerful groups or individuals ready to enforce their will on others. In other words a society in which tolerance is the highest good, far from remaining objectively tolerant, can easily become threatened by those who take advantage of a prevailing spirit of tolerance to impose their tyrannical or criminal will on the less powerful, and on those others with some vestige of an inclination to be law-abiding. Indeed the government itself can become frightened of antagonising such powerful groups and afraid of seeking to compel them to act in a spirit of toleration towards those who do not belong to the dominant groups or accept their hegemony.

There is an interesting parallel with the creation of the welfare state, whose authors were likewise very often men of high integrity and compassion. In *The Welfare State We're In*[1] James Bartholomew offers a compelling analysis of the consequences of state intervention to protect and promote citizens' welfare across the entire field of social action: health, education, provision for unemployment and support for citizens in their old age.

In the nineteenth and early part of the twentieth century there had been voluntary arrangements for social support which had been created and sustained by individuals, charities, friendly and philanthropic societies, and trade unions. The intentions of those who promoted the replacement of these with a centralised system controlled by national and local governments and funded through taxation, seemed laudible to many at the time. They believed that it would be more administratively tidy, and that there would be economies of scale, and less risk of some individuals or groups falling through the welfare net.

But the consequences have proved quite different from those which the original pioneers of this centralised welfare state intended and expected. Many aspects of the the current monolithic system are now failing badly, the social results have often proved disastrous, and the costs are in many cases now out of control.

An analysis similar to James Bartholomew's on the welfare state is now needed of the consequences of the past

1. See James Batholomew: *The Welfare State We're in*, London 2004.

encouragement of total moral freedom and the abandoning of restraints on social behaviour. Wiseman's recollections on what these two popes did to address the issues will help inform consideration of the balance to be struck between the role of the State and that of moral leaders in turning back the tide.

ANTONY MATTHEW

LEO THE TWELFTH

✶✶✶✶✶✶

CHAPTER I

HIS ELECTION

THE interval between the close of one pontificate and the commencement of another is a period of some excitement and necessarily of much anxiety. I remember being in Paris when Louis XVIII died, and Charles X succeeded to him. Chateaubriand published a pamphlet with the title, "Le Roi est mort, vive le Roi." There is no interregnum in successive monarchy: and that title to a book consists of words uttered by some marshal or herald, at the close of the royal funeral, as he first points with his bâton into the vault, and then raises it into the air.

But in elective monarchy, and in the only one surviving in Europe, there is of course a period of provisional arrangements, foreseen and pre-disposed. Time is required for the electors to assemble, from distant provinces, or even foreign countries; and this is occupied in paying the last tribute of respect and affection to the departed Pontiff. His body is embalmed, clothed in the robes of his office, of the penetential colour, and laid on the couch of state within one of the chapels in St Peter's, so that the faithful may not only see it, but kiss its feet. This last act of reverence to the mortal remains of the immortal Pius, the writer well recollects performing.

These preliminaries occupy three days: during which rises, as if by magic, or from the crypts below, an immense catafalque, a colossal architectural structure, which fills the nave of that basilica, illustrated by inscriptions, and adorned by statuary. Before this huge monument, for nine days, funeral rites are performed, closed by a funeral oration. For the body of the last Pope, there is a uniform resting-place in St. Peter's,—a plain sarcophagus, of marbled stucco, hardly noticed by the traveller, over a door beside the choir, on which is simply painted the title of the last Pontiff. On the death of his successor it is broken down at the top, the coffin is removed to the under-church, and that of the new claimant for repose is substituted. This change takes place late in the evening and is considered private. I cannot recollect whether it was on this or on a subsequent occasion that I witnessed it, with my college companions.

In the afternoon of the last day of the *novendiali*, as they are called, the cardinals assemble in a church near the Quirinal palace, and walk thence in procession, accompanied by their *conclavisti*, a secretary, a chaplain, and a servant or two, to the great gate of that royal residence, in which one will remain as master and supreme lord. Of course the hill is crowded by persons lining the avenue kept open for the procession. Cardinals never before seen by them, or not for many years, pass before them; eager eyes scan and measure them, and try to conjecture, from fancied omens in eye, or figure, or expression, who will shortly be the sovereign of that fair city, and, what is much more, the Head of the Catholic Church from the rising to the setting sun.

Equal they pass the threshold of that gate: they share together the supreme rule, temporal and spiritual: there is still embosomed in them all the voice yet silent, that soon will sound, from one tongue, over all the world, and the dormant germ of that authority which will soon again be concentrated in one man alone. Today they are all equal; perhaps tomorrow one will sit enthroned, and all the rest will kiss his feet; one will be sovereign, the others his subjects; one the shepherd, and the others his flock.

This is a singular and deeply interesting moment; a scene not easily forgotten. There pass before us men of striking figure, and of regal aspect. There is the great statesman of whom we have spoken, somewhat bowed by grief and infirmity, yet still retaining his brilliant gaze. There is the courteous, yet intrepid, Pacca; tall and erect, with a bland look that covers a sterling and high-principled heart: there, with snow-white head, and less firm step than his companion, is the saintly de Gregorio, lately a prisoner for his fidelity: Galeffi, less intellectual in features, but with a calm genial look that makes him a general favourite: Opizzoni, already till lately Archbishop of Bologna, who had boldly asserted the claims of papal, over those of imperial, authority, in a manner that had gained him imprisonment; beloved and venerated by his flock, admired at Rome, dignified and amiable in look. Many others were there whose names have not remained inscribed so deeply in the annals of the time, or retained their hold on the memory of its survivors. But there was one who no doubt entered as he came out, without a flutter of anxiety, when he faced the gate on either side. This was Odescalchi, young still, most noble in rank and in heart, with saintliness marked in his countenance, and probably meditating already his retreat from dignity and office, and the exchange of the purple robe for the novice's black gown. Many who preferred holiness to every other qualification, looked on his modest features with hope, perhaps, that they might soon glow beneath the ponderous tiara. But God has said, "Look not on his countenance, nor on the height of his stature. Nor do I judge according to the look of men; for man seeth the things that appear, but the Lord beholdeth the heart." [1]

Perhaps not a single person there present noticed one in that procession, tall and emaciated, weak in his gait, and pallid in countenance, as if he had just risen from a bed of sickness to pass within to that of death. Yet he was one holding not only a high rank, but an important office, and necessarily active amongst the population of Rome. For he

1. 1. Kings xvi.7.

was its Cardinal Vicar, exercising the functions of Ordinary. Nevertheless, to most he was a stranger: the constant drain of an exhausting complaint not only made him look blood-less, but confined him great part of the year to his chamber and his bed. Only once before had the writer seen him, on a day and in a place memorable to him,—St Stephen's feast, in the Papal chapel, in 1819.

Such was Cardinal Hannibal della Genga, whom a high-er election than that of man's will had destined to fill the Pontifical throne.

His previous history may be briefly told. He was the sixth of ten children of Count Hilary della Genga, and Mary Louisa Periberti, and was born at the family seat of Della Genga, August the 20th, 1760. He received his early educa-tion in a College at Osimo, from which he passed to one established in Rome for natives of the province whose name it bore, the *Collegio Piceno*. Thence, having embraced the ecclesiastical state, he entered the *Academia Ecclesiasti-ca*, an establishment already mentioned in the third chapter of our first book. The celebrated Cardinal Gerdil ordained him priest, on the 4th of June, 1783.

Pope Pius VI, visiting the house, and struck with his appearance, his manner, and the quickness of mind per-ceptible in his conversation, shortly took him into his household. In 1793, notwithstanding his youth and strong remonstrances, he was consecrated Archbishop of Tyre, by Cardinal de York, in the cathedral of Frascati; and sent as nuncio to Lucerne, whence in the following year he went to succeed the illustrious Pacca, in the important nunciature of Cologne.

In 1805, he became the subject of a grave contest between the Holy See and Napoleon. For the Pope named him extraordinary envoy to the German Diet, and the Emperor wished the Bishop of Orleans to be appointed. The Pope prevailed, and ordered the return of Monsignor Della Genga to Germany. He resided at Munich, and was there universally esteemed. In 1808, he was in Paris, engaged in diplomatic affairs on behalf of his sovereign; and, having witnessed, on returning to Rome, the treatment which he was receiving from his enemies, he retired to the abbey of Monticelli, which he held *in commendam*, and there devoted himself, as he thought for life, to the instruction of a choir of children, and the cultivation of music.

He was drawn from obscurity at the restoration, and deputed to present to Louis XVIII, at Paris, the Pope's letter of congratulation. This circumstance led to differences between him and Cardinal Consalvi, nobly repaired on both sides, when one had mounted the throne. But Della Genga returned from his mission of courtesy, with a health so shattered, and an appearance so altered, that people almost fled from him, and he thought seriously of returning to his abbey, where he had prepared his sepulchre, and secured its personal fit by lying stretched in its narrow cell.

However, in 1816, he was raised to the purple, and named Bishop of Sinigaglia. In 1820, he was appointed Vicar of Rome, and discharged the duties of his office with exemplary exactness, zeal, and prudence, till he occupied that highest office of which he had been deputy.[1]

While we have been thus sketching, hastily and imperfectly, one of many who passed almost unnoticed in the solemn procession to conclave,[2] on the 2nd of September, 1823, we may suppose the doors to have been inexorably closed on those who composed it. The conclave, which formerly used to take place in the Vatican, was on this occasion, and has been subsequently held in the Quirinal Palace.[3] This noble building, known equally by the name of Monte Cavallo, consists of a large quadrangle, round which

1. These details of Leo XII's earlier life are condensed from the *Histoire du Pape Léon XII* by the Chevalier Arnaud de Montor (two volumes).
2. English writers commit a common error by speaking of "the conclave," as meaning the body of cardinals assembled, on any occasion. The word is only applied to them when locked up together, for the election of the Pope. When assembled by him, they composes a "consistory."
3. The conclave has now been restored once more to the Vatican.

run the papal apartments. From this stretches out, along a whole street, an immense wing, its two upper floors divided into a great number of small but complete suites of apartments, occupied permanently, or occasionally, by persons attached to the Court.

During conclave these are allotted, literally so, to the cardinals, each of whom lives apart, with his attendants. His food is brought daily from his own house, and is examined, and delivered to him in the shape of "broken victuals," by watchful guardians of the *turns* and lattices, through which alone anything, even conversation, can penetrate into the seclusion of that sacred retreat. For a few hours, the first evening, the doors are left open, and the nobility, the diplomatic body, and in fact all presentable persons, may roam from cell to cell, paying a brief compliment to their occupants, perhaps wishing the same good wishes to fifty, which they know can be accomplished to only one. After that all is closed; a wicket is left accessible for the entrance of any cardinal who is not yet arrived; but every aperture is jealously guarded by faithful janitors, judges and prelates of various tribunals, who relieve one another. Every letter even is opened and read, that no communications may be held with the outer world. The very street on which the wing of the conclave looks is barricaded and guarded by a picquet at each end; and as, fortunately, there are no private residences opposite, and all the buildings have access from the back, no inconvenience is thereby created.

While conclave lasts, the administrative power rests in the hands of the Cardinal Chamberlain, who strikes his own coins during its continuance; and he is assisted by three cardinals, called the "Heads of Orders," because they represent the three orders in the sacred college, of bishops, priests and deacons. The ambassadors of the great powers receive fresh credentials to the conclave, and proceed in state, to present them to this delegation, at the *grille*. An address, carefully prepared, is delivered by the envoy, and receives a well-pondered reply from the presiding cardinal.

In the meantime, within, and unseen from without, *fervet opus*.[1] That human feelings, and even human passions, may find their way into the most guarded sanctuaries, we all know too well. But the history of conclaves is far from justifying the estimate made of them by many prejudiced writers. There will indeed be, at all times, diversities of opinions on matters of ecclesiastical and civil policy. For, in the former, where will be some who conscientiously desire things to be ruled with a strong hand, and corrected by severe measures, while others will be in favour of a more gentle pressure, and a gradual reform. Some will be inclined to yield more to the demands of the temporal power, and so prevent violent collisions; others will think it safer to resist every smaller encroachment that may lead to greater usurpations. It may even happen that a politico-ecclesiastical cause of division exists. These may consider Austria as the truest friend of religion, and best defender of the Church; while those may look on France as most earnest and powerful in attachment to the faith.

And it must, indeed, be further observed, that the election is of a prince as well as a pontiff, and that serious diversities of opinion may be held, relative to the civil policy most conducive to the welfare of subjects and the peace even of the world.

Thus, upon the three great divisions of papal rule, the purely ecclesiastical, the purely civil, and the mixed, there may be held, by men of most upright sentiments and desires, opinions widely different; and when choice must be made of one who has to work out his own principles, it is most natural that each elector will desire them to be in harmony with his own. But it is equally in conformity with ordinary social laws, that, in spite of personal peculiarities of ideas, men should combine in the unity of certain general principles;

1.[The work carries on briskly.] The quotation is from Virgil. Georgics IV,169.

and that some individuals, more energetic or more ardent than others, should become the representatives and leaders of all consentient with them, and so come to be reputed heads of parties, or even their creators.

Such divisions in opinion will be more deeply marked, and more inevitably adopted, after violent agitations and great changes, such as had distinguished the pontificate of Pius. The Church and the State had needed almost to be reorganised, after such devastation as had completely swept away the ancient landmarks. New kingdoms had arisen which literally effaced the outlines of old ecclesiastical juris-diction; and even what before had been a Catholic state had come under Protestant dominion. Conventual life and prop-erty had been annihilated in most of Europe; canon law had been abolished, church endowments had been confiscated; civil codes had been introduced at variance with ecclesiasti-cal jurisprudence; the authority of bishops had been deprived of all means of enforcing its decrees; in fine, a state of things had been produced totally different from what the Catholic world had ever before seen.

Many still alive remembered well the epoch antecedent to these changes, and formed living links with what had been, and what was justly considered, the healthy condition of the Church. They deplored the alteration; and they believed that too much had been conceded to the change-able spirit of the times. This would be enough to form a serious and deeply conscientious party, in the highest and best sense of the word. Others might just as conscientiously believe that prudence and charity had guided every portion of the late policy, and wish it to be continued under the same guidance. Without exaggeration, we may allow such conflicts of principle to have swayed the minds of many who entered the conclave of 1823; while there were others who had espoused no decided views, but had simply at heart the greatest general good, and reserved their final judgment to the period when they must authoritatively pro-nounce it. From such a condition of things it may happen that a papal election may apear like a compromise. The extreme views on either side must be softened; the intermediate party will do this. Two-thirds of the votes are required for a valid election. If this proportion could be commanded by one section, it would cease to be a party, and, therefore, where different opinions divided the body, a moderate view, more or less conciliatory, will prevail after a time; and the choice will probably fall on one who has lost the confidence of none, but who has not taken a prominent part in public affairs.

Such was, perhaps, the case in the election of Leo. That of the reigning Pontiff is an instance of unanimity and promptness without parallel.

It is not the purpose of this volume to describe the manner in which the business of the conclave is carried on. Suffice it to say, that twice a day the cardinals meet in the chapel contained within the palace, and there, on tickets so arranged that the voter's name cannot be seen, write the name of him for whom they give their suffrage. These papers are examined in their presence, and if the number of votes given to any one do not constitute the majority, they are burnt, in such a manner that the smoke, issuing through a flue, is visible to the crowd usually assembled in the square outside. Some day, instead of this usual sign to disperse, the sound of pick and hammer is heard, and a small opening is seen in the wall which had temporarily blocked up the great window over the palace gateway. At last the masons of the conclave have opened a rude door, through which steps the Cardinal Deacon, and proclaims to the many, or to the few, who may happen to be waiting, that they again possess a sovereign and a Pontiff. On the occasion of which we speak, the announcement ran as follows:

"I give you tidings of great joy; we have as Pope the most eminent and reverend Hannibal Della Genga, Lord Cardinal of the Holy Roman Church, Priest of the title of St Mary's beyond the Tiber, who has assumed the name of Leo XII."[1]

1. Although it is a well-known fact that a Pope on his accession takes a new name, by usage one already in the catalogue of his predecessors, it is

The news flew like electricity through the city, almost as quickly as the cannon's roar proclaimed it. This was on the 28th of September, after a short conclave of twenty-five days.

On the 5th of October the imposing ceremony of Leo's coronation took place. For the first time I then witnessed pontifical High Mass in St Peter's. All was new: the ceremony, the cirumstances, the person. As has been observed, the infirmities of Pius VII had prevented him from officiating solemnly; so that many of us who had already passed several years in Rome had not witnessed the grandest pontifical functions. But strange to say, though some of our body had shortly before received in his private oratory holy orders from his hands, as I had not enjoyed that privilege, the countenance, from which later I had to receive so many benign looks, was all but new to me. And the peculiar moment in which he stands painted, clear as an old picture, in my memory, was one that can be passed once only in each pontificate. As the procession was slowly advancing towards the high altar of the Vatican basilica, it suddenly paused; and I was but a few feet from the chair of state, on which, for the first time, the Pontiff was borne. No other court could present so grand and overpowering a spectacle. In the very centre of the sublimest building on earth, there stood around a circle of officers, nobles princes, and ambassadors in their dazzling costumes; and within them the highest dignitaries of religion on earth, bishops and patriarchs of the western and eastern Church; with the sacred college in their embroidered robes, crowned by heads which an artist might have rejoiced to study, and which claimed reverence from every beholder. But above them, on his throne, was he whom they had raised there, in spite of tears and remonstrances. Surely, if a life of severe discipline, of constant suffering, and of long seclusion had not sufficed to

not so generally known that, in the signature to the originals of Bulls, he retains his previous Christian name. Thus Leo XII would continue to sign himself as "Hannibal," and the present Pope signs "John" at the foot of the most important ecclesiastical documents. The form is: "*Placet Joannes.*"

extinguish ambition in his breast, his present position was calculated to arouse it. If ever in his life there could be an instant of fierce temptation to self-applause, this might be considered the one.

And wherefore this pause in the triumphant procession towards the altar over the Apostle's tomb, and to the throne beyond it? It is to check the rising of any such feeling if it presents itself, and to secure an antidote to any sweet draught which humanity may offer; that so the altar may be approached in humility, and the throne occupied in meekness. A clerk of the papal chapel holds up right before him a reed, surmounted by a handful of flax. This is lighted: it flashes up for a moment, dies out at once, and its thin ashes fall at the Pontiff's feet, as the chaplain, in a bold sonorous voice, chants aloud: *"Pater Sancte, sic transit gloria mundi."* "Holy Father, thus passeth away the world's glory!" Three times is this impressive rite performed in that procession, as though to counteract the earthly influences of the triple crown.

The Pope, pale and languid, seemed to bend his head, not in acquiescence merely, but as though in testimony to that solemn declaration; like one who could already give it the evidence of experience. His eye was soft and tender, moist indeed and glowing with spiritual emotion. He looked upon that passing flash as on a symbol which he deeply felt, as on the history of a whole pontificate—of his own—not long to read. But the calm serenity with which he seemed to peruse it, the sincere acceptance of the lesson stamped upon his features, allowed no suspicion of an inward feeling that required the warning. It seemed in most perfect harmony with his inmost thoughts.

CHAPTER II

YEARS of suffering, by lowering illness, had robbed the Pope, already in his sixty-fourth year, of many graces which adorned his earlier life. He appeared feeble and fatigued; his features, never strongly marked, wore upon them a sallow tinge, though the marks of age were not deeply engraven upon them. His eye, however, and his voice, compensated for all. There was a softness and yet a penetration in the first, which gained at sight affection and excited awe: which invited you to speak familarly, yet checked any impulse to become unguarded. And his voice was courteously bland, and winning; he spoke without excitement, gently, deliberately, and yet flowingly. One might hear him make severe remarks on what had been wrong, but never in an impetuous way, nor with an irritated tone.

On the occasion alluded to at the close of the last chapter, that look which had been fixed with a mild earnest gaze upon the "smoking flax," swept over the crowd, as the procession moved on; and I should doubt if one eye which it met did not drop its lid in reverence, or feel dim before the brighter fire that beamed on it. This at least was the impression which actual experience in that moment suggested.

But besides these pleasing characteristics, there was another, which admirably became his exalted position. This was a peculiar dignity and gracefulness, natural and simple, in his movements, especially in ecclesiastical functions. Being tall in person, the ample folds, and even somewhat protracted length of the pontifical robes gave grandeur to his figure, though his head might have been considered small; he stood conspicuous among his attendants; and he moved with ease, and yet with stateliness, from place to place. And then his countenance glowed with a fervent look of deep devotion, as though his entire being were immersed in the solemn rite on which he was intent, and saw, and heard, and felt nought else.

There were two portions of the sacred function to which I have alluded, that displayed these two gifts, differing immeasurably as they do in quality, but most admirably harmonising when combined. The first of these acts was the communion at that his first pontifical celebration, and the first ever witnessed by many. It is not easy to describe to one who has never witnessed it, this touching and overawing ceremonial. The person who has once seen it with attention and intelligence needs no description, he can never forget it.

In St Peter's, as in all the ancient churches, the high altar stands in the centre, so as to form the point from which nave, aisle, and chancel radiate or branch. Moreover, the altar has its face to the chancel, and its back to the front door of the church. Consequently the choir is before the altar, though, according to modern arrangements, it would look behind it. The papal throne is erected opposite the altar, that is, it forms the furthest point in the sanctuary or choir. Ample and lofty, it is ascended by several steps, on which are grouped, or seated, the Pontiff's attendants. On either side, wide apart, at nearly the breadth of the nave, are benches on which assist the orders of cardinals, bishops, and priests on one side, and deacons on the other, with bishops and prelates behind them; and then between them and the altar two lines of the splendid noble guard, forming a hedge to multitudes as varied in class and clan as were the visitors at Jerusalem, at the first Christian Whitsuntide. Then beyond rises truly grand the altar, surmounted by its sumptious canopy, which at any other time would lead the eye upwards to the interior of St Peter's peerless crown; the dome hanging, as if from heaven, over his tomb.

But not now. At the moment to which we are alluding, it is the altar which rivets, which concentrates, all attention. On its highest step, turned towards the people, has just stood the Pontiff, supported and surrounded by his ministers, whose widening ranks descended to the lowest step, forming a pyramid of rich and varied materials, but moving, living, and acting, with unstudied ease. Now in a moment it is deserted. The High Priest, with all his attendants, has retired to his throne; and the altar stands in its noble simplicity, apparently abandoned by the dignified servants. And yet it is still the object of all reverence. There is something greater there than all that has just left it. Towards it all look; towards it all bend, or kneel, and worship. There stand upon it, alone, the consecrated elements, on the paten and in the chalice. The sovereign Pontiff himself is nothing in their presence; he is a man, dust and ashes, there, in the presence of his Lord and Maker.

The Cardinal Deacon advances to the front of the altar, takes thence the paten, elevates it, and then deposits it on a rich veil hung around the neck of the kneeling Sub-deacon, who bears it to the throne. Then he himself elevates, turning from side to side, the jewelled chalice; and descending the steps of the altar, slowly and solemnly bears it, raised on high, along the space between the altar and the throne. A crash is heard of swords lowered to the ground, and their scabbards ringing on the marble pavement, as the guards fall on one knee, and the multitudes bow down in humble adoration of Him whom they believe to be passing by.

But at this first clebration, and coronation of the new Pope, there was a circumstance connected with this part of the function, that gave it, in the eyes of many, a special interest. The first Cardinal Deacon, to whom of right it belonged to assist the Pontiff in his function, was the ex-minister Consalvi. People who were unable to estimate a strength of character formed by better than worldly principles, were keenly alive to this singular coincidence. It was

sufficiently known that the two had not agreed on important matters; it was confidently reported that Consalvi had
opposed the election of Leo; it had been said, that before
then, at the Restoration in France, sharp words had been
addressed by the powerful minister to the prelate Della
Genga; and the public, or the world, or whatever it is
called, took it for granted that angry and even resentful passions must rankle in the hearts of both, and could not be
concealed, even near the altar which represented the Calvary of reconciliation. The one considered by the common
mind to have been trampled under foot, borne on the chair
of triumph; he who had humbled him walking by him as his
deacon,—what Lawrence was to Xystus[1];—surely this was a
position trying to human infirmity in both. No doubt it
would have been easy, had this been the feeling on either
side, to have escaped from such mutual pain.

As it was, we are told by the biographer of Leo, who
moved in a very different sphere from mine—in the diplomatic circle—that keen eyes and observant minds were
bent upon the Pontiff and his deacon, to trace some, even
casual, look of exultation, or of humiliation, in their respec-
tive countenances; but in vain. Even if they would have
"suffered anything human" at another time, each felt himself now engaged in the service of a higher Master, and held
his soul in full allegiance to it.

Without retaining the slightest recollection of having for
an instant looked at the sublime action of that moment
with any such profane thought, memory faithfully represents its picture. Calm, dignified, and devout, abstracted
from the cares of public life, forgetful of the world in which
he had moved, and utterly unconscious of the gazing thousands of eyes around him, advanced the aging minister, now
the simple deacon, with steady unfaltering step and graceful
movement. The man whom kings and emperors had hon-

1. Xystus was elected Pope in 257 AD and is known as Sixtus II. He was
martyred twelve months later in a persecution of the Emperor Valerian.
The maryrdom of the Deacon St Lawrence followed soon afterwards.

oured with friendship; from esteem for whom the haughty and selfish George of England[1] had broken thorugh all the bonds of premunire and penal statutes, and the vile etiquettes of 300 years, by writing to him; who had glided amidst the crowds of courts unflurried and admired; now shorn of power and highest office, is just as much at home in his dalmatic at the altar, and moves along unembarassed in his clerical ministry, with countenance and gait as becoming his place as though he had never occupied another. Many a one who had thought that Consalvi's natural post was the congress-hall of Vienna, or the banquet-room of Carlton House, would see in that hour that the sanctuary of St Peter's was as completely his home. He looked, he moved, he lived that day, as those who loved him could have wished; just as one would himself desire to do on the last day of his public religious appearance.

But the Pope himself, as he first rose, and then knelt at the Deacon's approach, must have defied the sharpest eye that sought in his a gleam of human feeling. Deep and all-absorbing devotion imparted a glow to his pale features; and, however his person might be surrounded by civil pomp and religious magnificence, it was clear that his spirit was conscious of only one single Presence, and stood as much alone as Moses could be said to be, with One other only besides himself, on Sinai. From the hand of his humble minister he received the cup of holiest love; their cheeks met in the embrace of peace; the servant too partook, as is described in the Pontifical Mass, from the same chalice as the master. Who can believe that, in that hour, they were not together in most blessed union?

After this, the new Pontiff was borne to the *loggia*, or balcony, above the door of St Peter's. and the triple crown was placed upon his head by the first Cardinal Deacon, the aged

1. George IV, then Prince Regent while his father, George III was suffering from one his bouts of mental incapacity, supported Cardinal Consalvi's diplomatic moves to restore the Pope's rule in the Papal States (see Wiseman's *Pius VII*, Fisher Press 2003.)

Albani. He then stood up to give his first solemn benediction to the multitudes assembled below. As he rose from his chair to his full height, raised his eyes, and extended his arms, then, joining his hands, stretched forth his right hand and blessed, nothing could exceed the beauty and nobleness of every motion and every act. Earnest and from the heart, paternal and royal at once, seemed that action which indeed was far more; for every Catholic there—and there were few else—received it as the first exercise in his favour of vicarial power from Him whose hands alone essentially contain "benediction and glory, honour and power."

The promises of the new reign were bright and spring-like. If the Pope had not taken any part in public affairs, if his health had kept him even out of sight, during previous years, he now displayed an intelligence, and an activity, which bade fair to make his pontificate one of great celebrity. But he had scarcely entered on his duties, when all the ailments of his shattered constitution assailed him with increased fury, and threatened to cut short at once all his hopeful beginings. Early in December he was so ill as to suspend audiences; before the end he was considered past recovery. In the course of January, 1824, he began to rally, against all hope. On the 26th of that month, I find the following entry in the journal before me:—"I had my first audience of Leo XII. He was ill in bed, as pale as a corpse, and much thinner than last year, but cheerful and conversable...I said, 'I am a foreigner, who came here at the call of Pius VII, six years ago;...my first patrons, Pius VII, Cardinals Litta, De Pietro, Fontana, and now Consalvi, are dead.' (here the Pope hung down his head, shut his eyes, and put his hand on his breast with a sigh. 'I therefore recommend myself to your Holiness's protection, and hope you will be a father to me, at this distance from my country.' He said he would," &c.

All Rome attributed the unexpected recovery to the prayers of a saintly bishop, who was sent for at the Pope's request, from his distant see of Macerata. This was Monsignor Strambi, of the Congregation of the Passion. He came immediately, saw the Pope, assured him

of his recovery, as he had offered up to heaven his own val-
ueless life in exchange for one so precious. It did indeed
seem as if he had tranfused his own vitality into the Pope's
languid frame. He himself died the next day, the 31st of
December,[1] and the Pontiff rose, like one from the grave.[1]

As he recovered, his character and his policy gradually
developed themselves. In the first a great simplicity, in the
second an active spirit of reform, were manifested. Of the
first quality, as exhibited in his personal habits, there will be
a better opportunity to say a few words. But it showed itself
in other ways. His reign, even taking into account its brief
duration, will appear less distinguished than those of his
predecessors, or successors, from the want of great public
works. This, however, is at least partly due to the quality
just mentioned in his character.

A peculiar feature in monumental Rome is the chronicle
which it bears on itself of its own history. Sometimes the
foreigner is pleased to smile, or to snarl, as his temper may
lead, at what he considers a pompous inscription on a
trumpery piece of work: a marble slab, in a ponderous
frame, to commemorate a spur or buttress in brick, reared
against an ancient monument. And yet, in several ways,
this has its uses. It is a traditional custom, which offers
many advantages. How do we trace out the history of an
ancient edifice so well as by the inscriptions found in, or
near, its ruins, which preserve the names of its restorers, or
those who added a portico or fresh decorations? How do we
recover its form and architecture so accurately, as from a
medal on which it has been represented, by the Emperor, or
family, that built, or repaired, or embellished it? How,
again, should we trace out the dark history of mediaeval
monuments, their destruction by time or fire, without the
rude verses and cramped tablets that run along them, or
hang upon them? And indeed little should we have known
of catacomb life and story, had the early Christians been

1. Vincent Strambi was a Passionist missioner before he became a Bishop.
He was canonised by Pope Pius XII in 1950. His feast day is 25 September.

less talkative in marble, and disdained to scratch the names of the dead and the feelings of the living in plaster or stone.

It is, therefore, the tradition of Rome to transmit "sermons in stone;" and as we are now thankful for the annals thus handed down to us from ancient times, let us be glad likewise that recent epochs have prepared similar advantages for remote posterity. The style, too, of such inscriptions follows the variations of taste, as decidedly as do the monuments on which they are carved. They are, in fact, themselves artistic monuments. It saves, moreover, much trouble to the visitor of a great city to see at once, written in large capitals upon the front of each lofty building, its names, age, founder, and use. He cannot mistake an hospital for the war office, nor an exchange for a court of justice. He learns to what saints a church is dedicated; and, if it possess an historical name, he at once seizes it.

Were London ever again to become a ruin, a few fragments of plaster might disclose the whereabouts of a dissenting chapel; and a queer old tablet might tell of some humble almshouses, founded by an eminent merchant. The remaining inscriptions would be the debris of shop-fronts and *facias* (whatever that means); with a few brass plates bearing the names of a dentist or a drawing master; or, what Lord Macaulay's sketchy New-Zealander might consider a leave for admission to some congenial fancy sports of cudgel or fist,—"Knock and Ring."

But, whether the practice be good or bad, Leo XII certainly did not adopt it. It was generally understood that he would not allow his name to be placed on any of his works. It was even said that, having visited some machinery on the roof of St Peter's for raising water thither, and being shown by Galeffi, the Cardinal archpriest of the church, an inscription recording that it was done in his pontificate, he desired it to be removed.

Some great works, indeed, were undertaken in his reign, but not finished; so that the glory which mankind usually awards to success is associated with other names. Yet should he be denied the merit of having commenced them? And after all, the daring required to plan and begin on a noble scale contains within it, or rather is, the germ of the untiring patience required to accomplish it. One of these vast enterprises was the rebuilding of the great Ostian basilica,[1] consumed by fire in the last days of his predecessor. It was soon discovered that no single portion of the edifice was secure, and that not a fragment of wall could be allowed to stand. Many were for merely covering the centre altar and tomb to be a Palmyra in the wilderness. But the Holy Father took a more generous view. In spite of an exhausted treasury, and of evil times, he resolved to begin the work of reconstruction on the original scale of the immense edifice which bore the name, in golden mosaic, of his holy patron, St Leo the Great. He appealed, indeed, to the charity of the faithful throughout the world, and he was generously answered. But the sums thus collected scarcely sufficed for preliminary expenses: those who, like myself, can remember the endless shoring up and supporting of every part of the fire-eaten walls, and the magnificent scaffolding that for strength would have borne an army, and for ease and security of access would not have imperilled a child, can easily imagine what treasures were spent before a stone was laid upon the ground.[2] But, in the meantime, the crow-bar and the mine were dislodging huge masses from Alpine quarries—the blocks of granite which were to form the monolith shafts of the giant columns for the nave and aisles in all four rows, besides the two, still more colossal, which the Emperor of Austria gave to support the triumphal arch leading to the sanctuary. Each, when shaped on the mountain-side, had to be carried down to the sea, embarked in a vessel of special construction, brought around Sicily into

1. Also known as St Paul without the Walls. See Chapter IX of Wiseman's *Pius VII* for an account of its destruction.

2. The architects in charge of the reconstruction were: Pasquale Belli, P. Bosio, P. Camporese and L. Poletti.

the Tiber, and landed in front of the church. But what the sub-
scriptions, however generous, did not reach, the munificence
of succeeding pontiffs has amply supplied. The work is now
finished, or nearly so[1]; and the collections that were made
form but a very secondary item in the budget of its execution.

Another great and useful work, not fully completed till
the reign of his second successor, was the repression of the
ravages committed by the Anio at Tivoli. That beautiful
river, which every traveller eagerly visits, to admire it, not
in tranquil course, but as broken and dashed to pieces in its
successive waterfalls, used to gain its celebrity at the
expense and comfort of the town through which it rushed.
The *praeceps Anio* often forgot its propriety, and refused to
do as the Thames was bid, "always keep between its banks."
As it pushed headlong towards the spot where the traveller
expected it, in the Sibyl's cave, boiling and torturing itself
with deafening roar, it would at times swell and burst its
bounds, sweeping away the houses that bordered it, with
road, wall, and bridge, not only hurling them below, but
bearing them into a huge chasm, in which it buried itself
underground. In the meantime, above the deep cold dell
into which you dive to see these mysteries of Anio's urn,
towers, like a pinnacle projected on the deep blue sky, the
graceful temple of the Sibyl[2]; raised high on a pedestal of
sharply cut rock, and seated on a throne of velvet verdure;
—that most exquisite speciment of art crowning nature, in
perfect harmony of beauties.

One of those traitorous outbreaks of the classical stream
occurred in November, 1826. It was more than usually

1. The transept was consecrated by Gregory XVI in 1840, and the
completed basilica by Pius IX in 1854.
2. The Temple is generally thought to have been originally dedicated to
the goddess Vesta. The building dates from the last years of the Roman
Republic. It is circular in construction; 10 of the original 18 Corinthian
columns survive. In medieval times it was converted into the Church of
Santa Maria della Rotunda. Wiseman does not mention that in 1828
there was a risk that it might be sold and transported to England!

destructive; and the ravages committed, and the damage inflicted, on the neighbouring inhabitants were beyond the reach of local resources. The Pope gave immediate orders for effectual repairs, on such a scale as would give security against future recurrence of calamity. A great deal was done; and, in October of the following year, he went, according to his practice, without giving notice, to inspect the progress of his works. It may well be imagined what delight this unexpected visit gave to the inhabitants of that poor, though industrious and beautiful city. They crowded around him, and accompanied him to the cathedral, where, after the usual function of benediction, he received in the sacristy the clergy and people of the place.

Later, it was found necessary to take a bolder and more effectual measure,—that of cutting a double and lofty tunnel through the hard travertine rock; and diverting the main stream before it reaches the town. The *cunicoli*, as they are called, form one of the grandest works of Gregory the Sixteenth's pontificate. They are worthy of Imperial Rome, bold, lofty, airy, and perfectly finished. Instead of having diminished the natural beauties of Tivoli, they have enriched it with an additional waterfall of great elevation; for they pour their stream in one sheet into the valley beyond; and when time shall have clothed its border with shrubs, and its stones with moss, it will not be easy to discern the hand of man, unless a well-timed and well-turned inscription records its author. One of the annual medals of Gregory's pontificate not only records but represents it.

Here are important undertakings on which the name of Leo might have been inscribed, had he so wished it. Nor was he behind his predecessors in attending to the usual and characteristic progress of whatever related to art. The library, the museum, excavations, and public monuments, were as studiously attended to, and as steadily improved or carried on, as at any other time; so that his pontificate was by no means a stagnant one; though records of its works may be sought in vain. Proofs of this will not be wanting as we proceed.

CHAPTER III

CONTINUATION

THE policy of the Pope manifested an active spirit of reform. This pervaded every part of his public government, from general administration to minute details. He placed the finances of the state under rigid administration, and brought them into such a condition, that he was early able to diminish taxation to no inconsiderable degree. Immediately after his coronation, he abolished several imposts; in March 1824 and January 1825, still further reductions were made in taxes which pressed unequally on particular classes. If I remember right, some of these abolitions affected materially the private revenues of the Pontiff. What rendered the reductions more striking was, that they were made in the face of considerable expenses immediately expected on occasion of the Jubilee. But so far from these having disturbed the equilibrium of the financial system, the Pope found himself able, at its close, that is, on January 1, 1826, to reduce the property-tax 25 per cent throughout his dominions.

As it was the heaviest and principal of all the taxes affecting land and whatever exists upon it, this measure was the removal of an universal burthen, and a relief to every species of industry and of capital.

It was generally understood that the Pope had another most highly beneficial measure in contemplation; and that, by the rigid economy of which his treasurer Cristaldi was the soul, he had nearly put by the whole sum requisite for its completion. This was the repurchase of the immense landed property in the Papal States, settled, with equity of redemption, by the Congress of Vienna, upon the family of Beauharnais. All this land, which had belonged to religious corporations, including many large and noble monastic edifices, in several fertile provinces of the north, had been given as a donation to Prince Eugene, with the remainder to his family. The inconveniences and evils resulting from this most arbitrary arrangement were numerous and manifest. Not only was a gigantic system of absenteeism established perpetually in the heart of the country, and a very large income carried abroad which otherwise would have been laid out on the spot; but an undue influence was created over a very susceptible population, by means of the widely scattered patronage held by the administrators of the property. In every greater town some spacious building contained the offices of the *Appannaggio*, as it was called; with a staff of collectors, clerks, overseers, land-surveyors, and higher officers; and in almost every village was a branch of this little empire, for managing the farms, and even smaller holdings of former communities. Many of the employed were, moreover, foreigners, whose religion was in declared antipathy to that of the natives, and whose morals neither edified nor improved the population.

To get rid of such an unnatural and anomalous state of things could not but be desirable for all parties. To the Papal government, and to the inhabitants of those provinces, it was a constant eye-sore, or rather a thorn in the side. An immense bulk of property, inalienable except in mass, mixed up with possessions of natives, checked the free course of speculation in land by exchange or purchase; and kept up the competition of resources, which were overwhelming, though far from well applied in cultivation and management. To the holder of the property its tenure must have been very unsatisfactory. Situated so far from his residence and his other estates, it had to be managed by a cumbrous and complicated administration, scattered over a broad territory; which, no doubt, swallowed up a considerable share of the profits.

It was, therefore, one of the objects of Leo's financial economy to redeem this valuable portion of his dominions from the hand of the stranger. Had his reign been prolonged a few years, he would probably have succeeded; but his successor occupied the throne for a period too brief to accompish much; and the revolution, which broke out at the very moment of Gregory's accession, soon absorbed the contents of the treasury, and threw into confusion the finance of the country for many years.

Still, at a later period (1845), this work was able to be accomplished. Under papal sanction a company was formed at Rome, in which the highest nobility took shares and direction, to repurchase the entire Apanage. Sufficient means were soon raised; the predetermined sum was paid; the country was cleared of the stranger power; and the property was easily sold to neighbouring or other proprietors, on equitable conditions. Gradual liquidation for the land and the stock on it was permitted, and thus many families have greatly increased their former possessions.

Besides improving so materially the financial state of his dominions, the Pope turned his attention to many other points of government. Soon after his accession he published a new code, or digest of law. This was effected by the *Motu proprio* of October 5, 1824, the first anniversary of his coronation. It is entitled *Reformatio Tribunalium*; and begins by mentioning that Pius VII had, in 1816, appointed a commission, composed of able advocates, to reform the mode of procedure; and that, on his own accession, he had ordered a thorough revision to be made of their labours. After great pains taken to correct and perfect it, it had been submitted to a congregation of Cardinals, and approved by them. The Pope adds, that he had been particularly anxious for the reduction of legal fees and expenses, and that he was ready to make any sacrifice of the public revenues, necessary to secure "cheap justice" to his subjects.

Education, in its highest branches, was another object of his solicitude. The Papal States contained several universities, besides other places of learning which partook of the nature and possessed the privileges of such institutions. By the Bull *Quod Divina Sapientia*, published on August 28, 1824, Leo reorganised the entire university system. The universities of Rome and Bologna composed the first class. Ferrara, Perugia, Camerino, Macerata and Fermo had universities of inferior grade. Those of the first class had thirty-eight, those of the second, seventeen chairs.

To take Rome as the example of the first class; it was composed of theological, medical, legal, and philosophical faculties, or colleges, as they are called in Italy; to which was added another with the title of the philological; and these were completely reconstructed. The philosophical college comprehended not only every branch of mathematics, but chemistry and engineering. A youth could offer himself for examination and receive degrees in this faculty. and so in the philological department, degrees could be taken in all the languages of which chairs exist there;—that is, in Greek, Hebrew, Syrio-Chaldaic, and Arabic. The members of the faculties were not merely professors of the university, but men eminent in the pursuits which they represented, in other institutions of the city, or even in private life.

A special congregation was created for the supervision of studies throughout the Papal States, under the title of "The Congregation of Studies;" to which belongs the duty of approving, correcting, or rejecting, changes suggested by the different faculties; of filling vacancies in chairs; and watching over the discipline, morals, and principles of all the universities and other schools.

It is certain that a new impulse was given to study by this vigorous organisation. Scholars from every part of Italy, and from other countries, not content with obtaining the annual prizes, studied for the attainment of degrees, which, besides being reputed honourable, formed a valuable qualification for obtaining chairs, or other preferment, at a distance. Among his former auditors, within the compass of two years, the writer can now reckon a Patriarch of

Jerusalem, a Bishop, a Vicar-General of a distingushed See, four professors in universities, and one at least in a great public institution. These he has come across or heard of since; others, from their sterling qualities, he has no doubt have advanced to high positions also.

But a more important improvement was made by this constitution. With the exception of a few theological professorships possessed, from a long period, by religious orders, all the chairs were thrown open to public competition.[1] On a vacancy by death or superannuation, notice was to be given, and a day appointed for examination in writing of such competitors as had sent in satisfactory testimonials of character. The only ground of exception and preference, was the having published such a work on the matter of the class, as might stand in the place of a mere examination paper, and such as proved the author's competency for the professorship to which he aspired.[2]. And, in addition to this, the Pope made the emoluments of the chairs better objects of ambition, by considerably increasing them. Indeed, he was most generous in providing means for the higher education of his subjects, lay and clerical. While he restored to the Society of Jesus the schools of the great Roman College, which had been carried on by secular clergy since the time of Clement XIV, he founded and endowed classes under superintendence of the latter at the old German College; where education begins almost with its very rudiments and reaches the highest point of ecclesiastical erudition.

It will be not uninteresting to add, that Leo XII ordered the works of Galileo, and others of a similar character, to be removed from the Index, in the edition published during his pontificate.

Speaking of church matters, it would be unjust to the memory of this Pope not to mention other improvements,

1. *Professores in posterum deligantur per concursum.* [Professors will in future be chosen by competition.] Tit.v.No.53.
2. Tit.v. No.70.

which were the fruit of his reforming spirit. He made a new adjustment of the parishes of Rome. There, as elsewhere, great inequalities existed in the labour, and in the remuneration, of parish priests. The richer quarters of the city, of course, were comparatively more lucrative than where all was misery; and yet the calls of charity were most urgent in the latter. Leo made a new division of parishes; of seventy-one existing parish churches he suppressed thirty-seven, some very small, or too near one another, and retained thirty-four. To these he added nine, making the total number forty-three. He moreover equalised their revenues; so that wherever the income of the parish priest did not reach a definite sum, considered necessary for a decent maintenance, this was made up from other sources guaranteed by the Government. Everyone must approve of this just reform. But it is only fair to add that nothing approaching to riches was thus provided. Ecclesiastical wealth is unknown in Rome, and the maintenance secured to a rector of a Roman parish would be treated as a sorry provision by a London curate.

There was an anecdote current at Rome, when this new circumscription was going on. The Pope, in his plans, intended the Chiesa Nuova to be a parish church. This belongs to the Fathers of the Oratory, founded, as all the world knows, by St Philip Neri. It was said that the superior of the house took, and showed to the Holy Father, an autograph memorial of the Saint to the Pope of his day, petitioning that his church should never be a parish. And, below it, was written that Pope's promises, also in his own hand, that it never should. This Pope was St Pius V. Leo bowed to such authorities, said he could not contend against two saints, and altered his plans.

Another ecclesiastical change introduced by him affected religious corporations. Besides the greater houses of different orders, there were several smaller communities of branches from them which seemed to be dying out, and in which it was difficult to maintain full monastic observance.

These he took measures gradually to suppress, by allowing the actual members to incorporate themselves with similar or cognate establishments; or, by receiving no more novices, gradually to be dissolved. Such a measure had of course its disapprovers; but certainly it was undertaken in a sincere spirit of enforcement to the utmost of religious observance.

It may interest many readers but little to learn the full extent which the reforming spirit of this Pontiff contemplated. Yet even those who affect indifference to whatever concerns Rome and its sovereign bishops, will not refuse evidence which proves, in one of them, the sincere and efficacious desire to amend abuses, even in matters apparently trifling.

Some of these reforms, certainly, were not inspired by any desire of popularity. They were decidedly unpopular, both with strangers and with natives.

For instance, he suppressed, for ever, one of the most singular and beautiful scenes connected with the functions of Holy Week. On the evening of Thursday and Friday, the church of St Peter used to be lighted up by one marvellous cross of light, suspended from the dome. This artificial meteor flung a radiance on the altar, where all other lights were extinguished, and even round the tomb of the Apostles, where, on one evening, certain rites are performed; it illuminated brightly the balcony under the cupola, from which venerable relics are exhibited; and it sent a flood of light along every open space, tipping every salient point and coigne with radiance, and leaving sharp-cut shadows beyond. It was such an effect of chiaroscuro—the most brilliant *chiaro* and the densest *oscuro*—as every artist loved to contemplate. But it was over-beautiful: it attracted multitudes who went only to see its grand effects. While pilgrims from the south were on their knees crowded into the centre of the church, travellers from the north were promenading in the wondrous light, studying its unrivalled effects; peeping into dark-some nooks, then plunging into them to emerge again into a sunshine that had no transition of dawn. And, doing all this, they talked and laughed, and formed chatting groups; then broke into lounging, saunter-ing parties, that treated lightly all intended to be most solemn. It made one sore and irritable to witness such con-duct; nay ashamed of one's home manners, on seeing well-dressed people unable to defer to the sacred feelings of others; bringing what used to be the behaviour of old "Paule's" into great St Peter's.

Unhappily for generations to come, it was considered impossible to check this disorder, except by removing its cause. The illuminated cross, which was made of highly burnished copper plates studded with lamps, disappeared, at the beginning of Leo's reign, by his orders; and, except when once renewed as a profane spectacle by the Republi-can leaders, it has been allowed to rest in the lumber-rooms of the Vatican.

In the two papal chapels raised seats had been long intro-duced, for the special accommodation of foreign ladies, who could thence follow the ceremonies performed at the altar. The privilege thus granted had been shamefully abused. Not only levity and disrespecful behaviour, not only gig-gling and loud talking, but eating and drinking, had been indulged in within the holy place. Remonstrance had been in vain, and so had other precautions of tickets and surveil-lance. One fine day, the ladies on arriving found the raised platform no more; the seats were low on the ground, suffi-cient for those who came to pray and join in the services, quite useless for those who came only to stare in wilful ignorance, or scoff in perverse malice.

This respect for God's house, the Pope extended to all other churches. In each he had a Swiss guard placed, to keep it in order, prevent artistic or curious perambulations at improper times, and assist in repressing any unbecoming conduct. Mod-esty of dress was also inculcated, and enforced in church.

These were not popular measures, and they made Pope Leo XII no favourite with travellers, who claimed a "right to do what they liked with" what was not "their own." But far beyond the suppression of what was generally popular like the luminous cross, went another measure, in exciting angry feelings among the people. Though, compared with other nations, the Italians cannot be considered as unsober, and the lightness of their ordinary wines does not so easily produce lightness of head as heavier potations, they are fond of the *osteria* and the *bettola*, in which they sit and sip for hours, encouraged by the very sobriety of their drink. There, time is lost, and evil conversations exchanged; there, stupid discussions are raised, whence spring noisy brawls, the jar of which kindles fierce passions and some-times deadly hate. Occasionally even worse ensues: from the tongue, sharpened as a sword, the inward fury flies to the sharper steel lurking in the vest or the legging; and the body, pierced by a fatal wound, stretched on the threshold of the hostelry, proves the deadly violence to which may lead a quarrel over cups.

To prevent this mischief, and cure the social and domes-tic evils to which the drink-shop, whatever it may sell, everywhere leads, the Pope devised the plan of confining them to what this word literally means. Wine was allowed to be *sold* at the *osteria*, but not allowed "to be drunk on the premises." Immediately within the door was a latticed parti-tion, through which wine could be handed out, and money taken in; but there was no convenience allowed for sitting, and but little for standing. This, it was hoped, would have induced men to take their refreshment home, and share it with their families. And so no doubt many did; while an end was put to drinking bouts, and the incentive of conver-sations to continue them, as well as to much strife and passion. It threw a portion of the crowd outside, instead of their being sheltered within; and created gatherings round the shop-door; but a sultry sun, or a sharp shower, or a cold winter's night, easily thinned them; and time would soon have soothed the first resentment which there gave itself vent. Nothing, however, could exceed the unpopularity of this measure, of establishing the *cancelletti*, as they were called; so that they were abolished immediately after the Pope's death.

These examples will show how little he valued the pleasant breeze of popular favour, in doing his duty. Some other actions of his will show how this sternness, in remedying or preventing the vices of the poor, was accompanied by kindness and charity. Soon after his accession, he had one evening finished his audiences, when he asked one of his domestic prelates, who lived out of the palace, and is now a cardinal, if his carriage was below. On his replying in the affirmative, the Pope said he would go out in it: put a cloak about him, descended by a private staircase, and accompanied by his noble attendant, drove to the School of the Deaf and Dumb, where an examination was being held. Such an event had never before been known, and we may imagine the delight and gratitude of pupils and teachers at this most unexpected surprise. He attended to the examinations, and then, with his own hands, distributed the prizes which he had brought with him.

This first instance was often repeated; but it was carried further, even to the lowest depths of misery. He visited the prisons; not only to inspect great improvements which he introduced into them, but to converse with their unfortunated inmates, and relieve their sufferings. In this manner he suddenly appeared at the debtors' prison in the Capitol, inquired personally into the cases of hardship, and discharged several prisoners, whose debts he took upon himself. The hospitals were unexpectedly visited, and their inmates consoled by the benign presence and soothing words of their holy Pontiff.

Anxious, however, to provide for the just and efficient administration of the charitable funds, many of which were mispent on worthless objects or wasted in the driblets of separate distributions, he appointed a Commission of high ecclesiastics and irreproachable laymen, to consolidate all the alms-funds of Rome, and to see their equitable distribution.

This noble institution, known as the *Congregazione dei Sussidi*, was organised by a Decree dated February 17, 1826. It is followed by a beautiful instruction to parochial committees, acting under this board, headed by a gentleman and a lady of charity, from among the parishioners. Nothing can be more sensible or more full of tender charity to the poor, than this truly episcopal and paternal address.

There was a community of Franciscan nuns, exceedingly edifying by their strict observance, miserably lodged in a steep narrow street behind the Quirinal, unable to keep enclosure from having no external church. The clergy of the English and Scotch colleges often ministered to their spiritual wants; and it has been the writer's privilege to do so. One day, in the very heat of the summer's afternoon, when everyone, nuns included, was taking the short repose of the time of day, the rough pavement of the lane quaked and rattled under the unusual dash and crash of horses and carriages. An impatient ring of the bell informed the community, who could not see into the street, that all this hubbub was on their account. "What is the matter? Who wants anything at this hour?" asked the aroused prioress. "The Holy Father is come to see you," was the answer. No doubt the Pope quietly enjoyed the fright, and joy, all in one, the amazement and confusion of the poor sisters, at this most unexpected proof of paternal care. He examined the house himself, and saw its inadequacy; and after familiarly and kindly conversing with them, departed, leaving them full of consolation.

There was an excellent and ample convent then unoccupied, near the beautiful fountain familiar to travellers by the name of Tartarughe, that is, Tortoises. It had every requisite for an enclosed community, and was attached to an elegant church, dedicated to St Ambrose, and supposed to occupy the site of his abode. This Leo had put into thorough repair and order; and when all was prepared, and the day was fixed for taking possession, the good ladies were waited upon by a number of ladies of the Roman nobility—always ready for such good actions,—and taken in their carriages to the Vatican, where a sumptious collation, as it appeared to them, was laid out for them; and they received the Pope's benediction, and enjoyed his amiable conversation, for a considerable time. They were then driven to their new home, whither their furniture had been removed. It was amusing to hear the nuns describe that day, —their bewilderment in going through the streets after years of seclusion; their bedazzlement and awe in the Vatican, and its church, which they visited; their delight at finding themselves in so spacious and convenient a house; their relief after a day harassing and toilsome to them, when their kind visitors had all left; and they closed their doors for ever to the outer world; then, lastly, their dismay at finding themselves without a morsel of food, sick and faint as they were, and unable, as they had been, through their confusion and reverence, to partake of papal refreshments. This alone had been overlooked; and only one nun, who surely deserved to take her place among the five wise Virgins of the parable, had brought a small basket of homely provisions, which she willingly shared with her famishing companions.

In this way did Pope Leo love to do good. He liked to take people by surprise, and see for himself; sometimes, it used to be said, with a very different result from that in the instance quoted.[1]

Before closing this chapter, it may be well to throw together a few more actions, which are connected with its subject, at least remotely, and which could not, perhaps, be so well introduced elsewhere.

1. A story used to be current, the truth of which cannot here be vouchsafed for, of his driving, at the same unreasonable hour, to a church of a religious community of men, supposed to be not well kept. He was in it before the members of the house were roused, and knelt at the plain bench or *genuflessio*, before the altar. He then entered the house, and conversed affably as usual. As he left, a delicate request was made for some memorial of his visit. He replied that he had left one where he had knelt. On going thither they found LEO XII, written on the dust which covered the *prie-dieu*.

Having mentioned his attention to the progress of art, as in harmony with the conduct of all his great predecessors, it may not be amiss to specifiy one or two instances. The Vatican library is indebted to him for very valuable additions. The principal one, perhaps, is the Cicognara collection of works relative to art. The nobleman, whose property it was, is well known for a magnificent history of sculpture; a work which united his name with those of Winkelmann and Agincourt. For the compilation of this book, he had naturally collected most valuable and expensive works on every department of art. At his death, this collection was for sale. It was purchased by the Pope, and given to the Vatican library. Besides this, he added many thousands of volumes to its rich stores, so that new rooms had to be incorporated in its immense range. The classical department particularly was increased.

It was during this pontificate also that the germ of the new splendid Etruscan museum was formed; for the excavation and study of the city of the tombs, which still remains on the border of Tuscany, belonging to the old Etruscan towns, were peculiarly carried on under this Pope.[1]

He showed himself, indeed, quite as great a patron of art as any of his predecessors; but he was most anxious that morality should not be compromised by it. A group of statues in the new gallery erected by his predecessor disappeared after his first visit, as did gradually other pieces of ancient sculpture offensive to Christian modesty. When a magnificent collection of engravings representing Canova's works had been prepared he purchased the plates at an immense cost, I believe at Florence; that he might suppress and destroy such as were not consistent with delicacy of morals.

1. During Leo's reign Giambattista Vermiglioli pushed forward the excavation of Etruscan sites in Perugia where the latter held the University chair in archaeology. In 1827 the bishop of Corneto entrusted the task of surveying the recently discovered Etruscan tombs in his diocese to two eminent Germans. The international Instituto di Correspondenza archaeologica was founded in Rome in 1829.

Among his works must not be forgotten one which is commemorated on one of his annual medals,—the beautiful baptistery of Santa Maria Maggiore, adorned with the richest marbles, and constructed with exquisite taste.

And in conclusion, as illustrative of his good nature and kindness, I will mention a singular visit which he one day unexpectedly received. It is well known that ladies are not admitted into the portion of the palace occupied by the Pope. He leaves his apartment for the museums or the library when he receives them. During hours of general audience the state rooms present an appearance of considerable state. Each of them has its body of guards, more for becoming appearance than for any effectual services; and chamberlains, clerical and lay, are in attendance in the inner chambers, as other classes of officers are in the outer. But soon after twelve all this formal court diappears; silence and solitude reign through the papal apartments. Still the person of the sovereign is not so badly and weakly guarded as that of Isboseth, the son of Saul, whose only portress used to nod over the tray of corn which she was cleaning. Below, indeed, there is a guard of Swiss, which might allow any one to pass: but at the foot of the staircase of the palace is a sentinel, and in the great hall is a small guard in attendance. This would be difficult to pass; for the next room is the first of the pontifical apartments, occupied only by a few servants, who, in the warm hours of the day, might easily be dozing.

Be all this as it may; certain it is that one afternoon it was announced to the Pope that a lady had made her way past the guard and had penetrated far, before she was discovered, into the *penetralia* of the palace. She had of course been stopped in her progress, or she might have found herself suddenly in the presence chamber, or rather in the study usually occupied by the Pontiff at that hour. What was to be done with her? was asked in dismay. Such an act of presumption had never before been known; there was a mystery about her getting in: and this was all the more difficult of solution, because the intruder could not speak Italian, and it could only be collected that she desired to see the Pope. Let it be remembered that secret societies were then becoming alarmingly rife, and that domestic assassination of persons in high places had been attempted, occasionally with success. The Pope apprehended no such danger, and desired the adventurous lady to be admitted at once. He gave her a long audience, treating her with his usual kindness. She was an American woman, who had been seized with a strong charitable desire to convert the Pope from what she considered his errors, and had thus boldly and successfully attempted to obtain a conference with him. That she did not change the Pope is certain; but that her opinion of him was changed there can be no doubt. For she must have been charmed with the gentleness and sweetness, as well as the nobleness and dignity, of his mien and speech.[1]

1. It was from Cardinal Pacca at the Villa Clementina that we heard this anecdote; and he mentioned that the Pope had asked her if she had not believed him to have a cloven (or ox's) foot; but she, halting between her courtesy and truthfulness, hesitated to answer, especially as she had given furtive glances towards the hem of the papal cassock. On which the Pope good-naturedly convinced her that he was clearly shod on human and Christian principles. The Cardinal added that, in his travels, some Protestants in conversation with him did not deny his belief in that pious and orthodox tradition; upon which Pacca wittily observed, "If you believe that the Pope to be graced with a goat's foot, you must naturally expect us cardinals to be garnished with a kid's. This you see, is not my case."

Leo had in his apartments a faithful companion, in the shape of a most intelligent little dog. After his death, it was obtained by Lady Shrewsbury, with whom many will remember it.

CHAPTER IV

THE JUBILEE

THE great event of this pontificate undoubtedly was the Jubilee of 1825. The first historical celebration of this festival was in 1300; though it was then said that vague tradition recorded a similar observance, of the first year in the previous century. It seems as if the spontaneous rush of pilgrims to Rome took place at the beginning of 1300; for the Bull by which it was regulated was not issued till the 21st of February. Boniface VIII decreed that this should be a centenary feast; Clement VI, in 1342, reduced the interval to 50 years; then it was further brought down to twenty-five. On this plan it was regularly continued for three centuries, till 1775, when Pius VI celebrated the Jubilee proclaimed by his predecessor the year before.

The regularity of period naturally produced a systematic mode of proceeding, and regular provisions for its good order. Accordingly, the practice has been, that on Ascension Day of the proceeding year, the Pope promulgates the Holy Year, or Jubilee. On Christmas Eve, he proceeds in state to the great portico of the Vatican basilica; which, though only a vestibule, must needs be of great dimensions, to afford a place for such ceremonials, and the thousands who flock to witness it.

The visitor to Rome may easily have noticed, that, of the five great doors opening from the porch into the church, the one nearest to the palace is walled up, and has a gilt metal cross upon it, much worn by the lips of pilgrims. On enquiry, he will be told that it is the *Porta santa*, or "Holy Gate," like the "King's Gate" at Jerusalem,—never to be opened except for most special entrance. Only during the year of Jubilee is this gate unclosed; and it is for the purpose of opening it, as symbolical of the commencement of the Jubilee, that the Pope has descended to the vestibule. The immense church is empty, for the doors have been kept closed all day; an innumerable multitude, beginning with royal princes and descending to the poorest pilgrims from Southern Italy, eagerly wait in the portico and on the steps without. After preliminary prayers from Scripture singularly apt, the Pope goes down from his throne, and, armed with a silver hammer, strikes the wall in the door-way, which, having been cut round from its jambs and lintel, falls at once inwards, and is cleared away in a moment by the active *Sanpietrini*.[1]

The Pope, then, bare-headed and torch in hand, first enters the door, and is followed by the cardinals and his other attendants to the high altar, where the first vespers of Christmas Day are chaunted as usual. The other doors of the church are then flung open, and the great queen of churches is filled. Well does the ceremonial of that day remain impressed on my memory; and one little incident is coupled with it. Among the earliest to pass, with every sign of reverence and devotion, through the holy gate, I remember seeing, with emotion, the first clergyman who in our times had abandoned dignity and ease as the price of his conversion. He was surrounded by his family in this pilgrim's act, as he had been followed by them in his "pilgrimage of grace." Such a person was rare in those days, and indeed, singular: we little thought how our eyes might become accustomed, one day, to the sight of many like him.

1. These are the body of workmen of "every arm," retained in regular pay by St Peter's, and wearing a particular dress. They keep the church in its perfect repair and beautiful condition almost without external help. Their activity and intelligence are quite remarkable.

Some reader may perhaps ask, in what, after all, consists the Jubilee? What are its duties, and what its occupations? A Catholic easily understands this. It is a year in which the Holy See does all it can to make Rome spiritually attractive, and spiritually only. The theatres are closed; public amusements are suspended; even private recreations pressed within the bounds of Lenten regulations. But all that can help the sinner to amendment, or assist the devout to feed his faith and nourish his piety, is freely and lavishly ministered. The pulpit is occupied by the most eloquent preachers, awakening the conscience or instructing ignorance; the confessionals are held in constant possession by priests who speak every language; pious associations or confraternities receive, entertain, and conduct from sanctuary to sanctuary the successive trains of pilgrims; the altars are crowded by fervent communicants; while, above all, the spiritual remission of temporal punishment for sin, known familiarly to Catholics under the name of an Indulgence, is more copiously imparted, on conditions by no means over easy. Rome, during that year, becomes the attracting centre of Catholic devotion; the magnet which draws it from every side. But it does not exhaust it or absorb it; for multitudes go back full of gratitude to Heaven and to the Holy See for the blessings which they feel they have received, and the edifying scenes in which they have been allowed to take part.

However, before endeavouring to recall to memory a few of these, it may be well to describe some of the preparations for them. To the Pope's own resolute and foreseeing mind alone, perhaps, was due the Jubilee of 1825. There should naturally have been one held the first year of the century. But the calamities of the times, and the death of Pius VI, had effectually prevented its observance.

Leo intimated his intention to proclaim it in due course, for its proper year; but met only opposition on every side. At home, his Secretary of State feared the introduction into the provinces and into Rome of political conspirators and members of secret societies; who, under the cloak of the pilgrim's scalloped cape, might meet in safety to plot destruction.

The Treasurer was terrified at the inroad which extra expenses would make into his budget, and protested against financial embarassments that he foresaw would ensue. Yes, reader! Marvel not! You have possibly been taught that a Jubilee is one of the happiest devices of Roman astuteness for filling an exhausted exchequer; a sort of wholesale barter for temporal goods, of those spiritual goods, which are usually dealt in retail only! If such has been the doctrine taught you, and believed by you, may you, if nothing else will undeceive you, live till next Jubilee, and have heart to visit it, and satisfy youself with your own eyes, whether Rome be the giver or the receiver; on which side turns the balance of accounts between the prodigality of her charity and the indigence of her clients. But we shall see.

From abroad, immeasurable difficulties were raised. Naples was naturally the power most interested in the coming festival, both from the proximity of the place, from traditional feelings, and for the easy propensity of its population to abandon home, either in quest of labour or for pilgrim purposes. Its minister was instructed to raise every difficulty, and even to engage the representatives of foreign powers in active opposition. Austria, still under the influence of Josephine ideas,[1] was at best cold: and the German Protestant powers, declared open hostility. Yet in the face of all these obstacles, Leo's only answer was, "Nevertheless the Jubilee shall be!" And it was.

On Ascension Day he issued the Bull of preparation, clear, bold, and cheering, as a silver clarion's note. Seldom

1. A reference to Joseph II. Son of Emperor Leopold he became sole ruler of the Holy Roman Empire in 1780 on the death of his mother, Maria Theresa. Much influenced by the ideas of the enlightenment, he was strogly anti-clerical, and hence his relations with the Papacy were strained. He abolished numerous religious communites, particularly those not engaged in corporal works, extended religious toleration to Uniates, Protestants, Orthodox and Jews. Civil marriage and divorce were permitted; capital punishment abolished; freemasonry flourished. He died in 1790.

has a document proceeded even from the Holy See more noble and stately, more tender and paternal. Its language, pure, elegant, and finely rounded, flows with all the greatness of Roman eloquence; yet in tone, in illustration, and in pathos, it is thoroughly Christian, and eminently ecclesiastical. It speaks—as only a Pope could speak, with a consciousness of power that cannot fail, and of authority that cannot stray. Its teaching is that of a master, its instructions that of a sage, its piety that of a saint.

The Pope first addresses every class of men who recognise his spiritual sovereignty; entreating kings to put no hindrance in the way of faithful pilgrims, but to protect and favour them, and the people readily to accept his fatherly invitation, and hasten in crowds to the banquet of grace spread before them. Then, after having warmly exhorted those who, in addition, recognise his temporal dominion, he turns to those who are not of his fold, those even who had persecuted and offended the Holy See; and in words of burning charity and affectionate forgiveness he invites them to approach him and accept him as *their* father too; and his words bring back the noble gesture with which he threw open his arms, when he gave his first public benediction, and seemed to open a way to his heart for all mankind, and press them to it in tender embrace.

From the moment this decisive document was issued, some preparations were begun, and others were more actively pursued. The first class of these preliminaries were of a religious character. *Missioni*, or courses of stirring sermons, calling on sinners to turn from their evil courses, were preached, not merely in churches but in public squares—for the churches did not suffice—so as to cleanse the city from sin, and make it a holy place for those who should come to seek edification there. In the immense and beautiful square known to every traveller as Piazza Navona, a concourse of 15,000 persons was said to be present, when the Pope, on the 15th of August, went to close these services by his benediction. It required stentorian lungs to address such a crowd, and be audible; fortunately these were to be found, in contact with a heart full of goodness and piety, in the breast of Canonico Muccioli. When this zealous man died, still young, a few years later, hundreds of youths belonging to the middle classes, dressed in decent mourning, followed in ranks their friend to his sepulchre. The same tribute of popular affection was exhibited later still, in 1851, to the amiable and edifying Professor Graziosi.

But to return; the Pope took many by surprise, when they saw him, opposite, listening, from the apartments of the Russian Embassy in the Pamphili palace, to the Canon's closing sermon. Thence he descended, accompanied by his heterodox host and admirer, the Chevalier Italinski, to a throne erected for him in the open air.

In addition to this spiritual preparation, material improvements were not forgotten. A visitation of churches, oratories, and all religious institutions had been begun, in virtue of which all irregularities in their arrangements were corrected, dilapidations repaired, ornaments restored, and old or decayed objects renewed. Considerable expense was thus incurred by some of the greater, and older, basilicas.

But more serious still were the preparations necessary to lodge and feed the crowds of pilgrims who were expected. To prevent any alarm on this head, on the part of foreign princes, the Pope sent word to the embassies that he did not wish them to make any provision for their poor countrymen, as he took on himself this duty of hospitality. He observed that he would rather pawn the church plate of Rome, than be wanting in its discharge.

There is in Rome a large house, attached to a Church of the Holy Trinity, expressly established for the charitable entertainment of pilgrims. Hence it is called *La Trinità dei pellegrini*. It is divided into two sides, one for men and the other for women. The ground floor is laid out in immense refectories, above which are dormitories equally vast. During the Holy Week there is a certain amount of activity in the house; as a considerable number of pilgrims then arrive, perhaps half a refectory, and half a dormitory, may be occupied. During the rest of the year, the establishment sends a huge carriage, now rather modernised, to the hospitals, to bring away all discharged patients; to whom, under the titles of convalescents, it gives three days' hospitality, and often, leisure to look out for some occupation.

The revenues of the house, the fruit of charity, are tolerably abundant; and it used to be said that, in the interval between the two jubilees, they were employed, the first half of the time in paying off the liabilities incurred, and the second in accumulating for the coming celebration. But, in addition to the accommodation permanently secured at home, the charity provided immense lodging room along the wide and airy corridors of religious houses. In the month of November, our confraternity of the Holy Trinity, to which many English belong, lodged and fed for three days 23,090 men and 15,754 women, in all 38,844 persons; besides 350 members of branch confraternities. From this some idea may be formed of the scale on which hospitality was exercised during the entire year.

The order observed was the following. The pilgrim, on his arrival at the house, had his papers of pilgrimage examined, and received his ticket of hospitality. In the evening the new comers were brought into a hall surrounded by raised seats, and supplied with an abundant flow of hot and cold water. Then, after a short prayer, the brothers of the confraternity, or the sisters in their part of the house, washed their feet, way-worn and sore by days or weeks of travel; and the ointment of the apothecary, or the skill of the surgeon, was at hand to dress wounds and bandage sores. This was no mere ceremony, no symbolical rite; but one saw and felt how in olden times "to wash the feet of the saints," when they asked for a night's harbour, was a real act of charity worthy of the Christian widow. It was evidently an exquisite relief to the jaded wayfarer.

Thus refreshed, the pilgrims joined the long procession

to supper. A bench along the wall, and a table before it, railed off to prevent the pressure of curious multitudes, were simple arrangement enough; but the endless length of these, occupied by men of every hue, and many languages, formed a striking spectacle. Before each guest was his plate, knife, fork and spoon, bread, wine and dessert. A door in each refectory communicated with a roomy hall, in which huge cauldrons smoked with a supply of savoury soup sufficient for an army. This was the post of honour; a cardinal or nobleman, in the red course gown and badge of the brotherhood, with a white apron over it, armed with a ladle, dispensed the steaming fluid into plates held ready; and a string of brothers, at arm's length from one another all round the refectory, handing forward the plates with the alacrity of bricklayers' labourers, soon furnished each hungry expectant with his reeking portion. Two additional rations were served out in the same manner. The guests fell to it with hearty good will, and generally showed themselves right good trencher-men.

Opposite each stood a serving man, who poured out his wine, cut his bread, changed his portions, and chatted and talked with him. Now these servitors were not hired, but all brethren of the confraternity; sometimes a royal prince, generally some cardinals, always bishops, prelates, noblemen, priests, gentry, and artificers.

Then, occasionally, a sudden commotion, a wavy movement through the crowd, would reach the outer door along the passage to the lavatory, just as prayers were beginning. All understood what it meant. The Holy Father was coming without notice. Indeed none was required; he came simply to do what everyone else was going to do; only he had the first place. He knelt before the last line of pilgrims, taking his chance of who it might be. If any priest were in the number, he was naturally placed first; and he would probably feel more sensitively than a dull uneducated peasant, the honour, not unmixed with humiliation, of having so lowly an office discharged in his person, by the highest of men on earth. And then, he would find himself waited on at table, by that master who coming suddenly in the night upon his servants, and finding them watching, knows how to gird himself, and passing along, ministers to them.

It was said that among the poor pilgrims came in disguise persons of high rank, who, after they had passed their triduum of charity among the poorest, faring as they, and receiving the cup of water as disciples in Christ's name, resumed their place in society, and remained in Rome as visitors, without any indelicate recognition. It was whispered that one couple, a German and his wife, were even of higher blood. Indeed, I remember one used often to remark, that the elegant language, the polished manners, and the half-easy, half-embarassed air of some pilgrims, bespoke a different class from that of the general run. But one thing was very noticeable on this as on other occasions—the naturalness, and absence of embarassment (so well-expressed in Italian by *disinvoltura*), with which these poor people received the attentions of persons whom they knew to be of such superior station, civil or ecclesiastical. While they allowed all menial services to be performed for them, without awkward bashfulness, or any attempts to prevent it, they accepted them with an humble thankfulness and a natural grace that showed how clearly they appreciated the motive which prompted their being rendered. They manifestly understood, that not merely to them, but to Him also whom the poor represent, were they offered.

Supper ended, and its baskets of fragments for the morning's breakfast put by, the long file proceeded up-stairs to bed singing one of the short religious strains in which all Italians can join; a sort of simultaneous yet successive chorus, winding along, stunning to your ears at the spot where you chanced to stand; alternately swelling and fading away, as it came from one or other side of the stairs; then dying away in the deep recesses of the dormitory above, yet seeming to be born again and grow at the beginning of the line still unemerged from the supper hall.

During the day, the pilgrims were conducted in bands from sanctuary to sanctuary; were instructed at stated times; were directed to the performance of their higher religious duties, by frequenting the Sacraments; and at the close of the three days were dismissed in peace, and returned home, or remained in the city at their own charge.

The Holy Father was the soul of all this work. To see him, and carry back his blessing, was of course one of the most highly coveted privileges of a pilgrimage to Rome. Hence he had repeatedly to show himself to the crowds, and bless them. They were instructed to hold up whatever they wished to have blessed; and certainly scarcely ever did Rome present a more motley crowd, arrayed in every variety of costume, from the sober, and almost clerical, dress of the German peasant, to the rainbow hues of the Abruzzi or Campania.

But the Pope manifested his hearty sympathy in his Jubilee by a more remarkable proof than these. He daily served in his own palace twelve pilgrims at table; and his biographer tells us that he continued this practice throughout his reign. To his accompanying them I well remember being an eye-witness. For one of such delicate health and feeble frame it was no slight undertaking to walk from the Vatican to the Chiesa Nuova; but to perform this pilgrimage bare-foot, with only sandals on his feet, was more than any one was prepared for. He was preceeded by the poor, surrounded and followed by them. Tears flowed on every side, and blessings were uttered deep and warm. His look was calm and devout, and abstracted from all around. It reminded every one forcibly of St Charles at Milan,[1] humbling himself by a similar act of public devotion, to appease the Divine wrath manifested in the plague.

It must not be thought that the celebration of the Jubilee monopolised the attention of the Pope. No year of his reign was more actively occupied than this with important affairs, especially abroad. But one great beneficial

1. S Charles Borromeo (1534-84).

improvement within may be traced to this "holy year." The Pope was determined that the roads would be safe for his poor pilgrims, and took such active measures, in concert with neighbouring states, that the system of brigandage was completely extinguished.

The last act, however, of its destruction deserves recording. A good old priest, the Abbate Pellegrini, the Archpriest of Sezze, ventured alone to the mountains which formed the head-quarters and stronghold of the *banditti*, unauthorised and uninvited. Without pass-word except the expression of his charity; without a pledge to give, that his assurances would be confirmed; without any claim, from position, to the fulfilment of his promises, he walked boldly into the midst of the band, and preached to them repentance and change of life. They listened: perhaps they knew that active measures were being planned for their extermination; more probably the very simplicity and daring of the feeble unarmed peace-maker touched their rude natures, and they wavered. But they were among the most dreaded of their race, nay, the most unpardonable, for some of them had been the assassins of the Terracina students.[1] One of them was their chief, Gasparone, who owned the commission of many murders. What hope could they entertain of pardon? The old man took upon himself to give his priestly word that their lives would be spared: they believed that word, and surrendered to him at discretion. The city of Sezze was astonished at beholding this herd of wolves led in by a lamb. All admired the heroic action, the self-devoting charity of this worthy ecclesiastic, who sought no reward, and who might have received a bullet or a stab for his first welcome from those desperadoes, but who had done in a few hours what troops and statesmen, in combined action, had not been able to effect in years. His word was respected, his promise fulfilled; and these brutal men are dying out their lives of expiation in

1. An account of this is in Chapter X of Wiseman's *Pius the Seventh* (Fisher Press, 2004).

the fortress of Città Vecchia.

Before closing this chapter it may not be out of place to add a few words on a subject connected with the Jubilee. The college, so long the writer's home, where he gathered the recollections embodied in this volume, owed its existence to this religious institution. It is true that the Saxon King Ina had opened a home to his countrymen visiting the shrine of the apostles; and this was continued in after ages. Still nothing like an hospice for English pilgrims existed till the first Jubilee, when John Shepherd and his wife Alice, seeing this want, settled in Rome, and devoted their substance to the support of the poor palmers from their own country.[1] This small beginning grew into sufficient importance for it to become a royal charity; the King of England became its patron, and named its rector, often a person of high consideration. Among the fragments of old monuments scattered about the house by the revolution, and now collected and arranged in a corridor of the college, is a shield surmounted by a crown, and carved with the ancient arms of England, lions or lionceaux, and fleur-de-lis, quarterly. This used formerly to be outside the house, and under it was the following quaint inscription, the original of which is lost. A copy, however, of it has been obtained from old transcripts, and is painted under the arms, in the original character—

"Haec conjuncta duo
Successus debita legi
Anglia dant, regi,
Francia signa suo."

Laurentius Chance me fecit
m.cccc.xij

1. In this Jubilee several English pilgrims are supposed to have perished by an accident on the bridge of St Angelo. A mule kicking in the crowd caused pressure against the wooden parapets, which gave way, and a great number of persons were precipitated into the river and drowned.

Which may be rudely translated—

> "These arms, whose award
> From succession springs
> France with England brings
> To their common Lord."

Laurence Chance executed me
1412

In the archives of the college are preserved the lists of the pilgrims who, from year to year, visited Rome; and as the country or diocese from which they came is recorded, they are valuable documents, consulted for local or family history. Many of the pilgrims were youths of good connections, students at Bologna, who, in their holidays, chose to visit Rome as pilgrims *in forma pauperum*, and received hospitality in the "English hospital of St Thomas." This was extended to a longer period than is granted to Italian pilgrims. Many other nations had also their hostelries to receive their countrymen, especially at those periodical seasons when

> "...longen folk to goon on pilgrimages,
> And palmeres for to seken straunge strondes."[1]

The rupture of Henry VIII with the Holy See put an end to the influx of pilgrims from England to Rome; and arrivals pretty nearly ceased under Elizabeth. In the meantime three different establishments had been united,—those of the Holy Trinity, of St Thomas, and of St Edward,—on the spot where our present college stands; and a church had been built, the great altarpiece of which, yet preserved, commemorated the formation of this coalition. A bishop, and several other refugees for the

1. Geoffrey Chaucer The Canterbury Tales, The Prologue, l. 12.

faith, lived there, till Gregory XIII, in 1579, converted the hospital into a college, as then more needed, with the condition that should the religious position of England ever change, the institution should return to its original purpose. May the happy omen be accomplished, but without any necessity for its proposed consequence!

The mention of this place naturally awakens recollections, in which it is associated with the principal subject of this work. The English College and Leo XII blend together in pleasing harmony among the remembrances on which the writer can look back most gratefully.

CHAPTER V

THE POPE AND THE ENGLISH COLLEGE

THESE recollections commenced in 1818;[1] the great event of the Jubilee brings us down to 1825. This is a long interval in the spring of life. The obscure and noiseless duties of youth must, during such an interval, work a change in mind, in feeling, in habits, perhaps in state. So it was here. The aim of years, the goal of long preparation, the longed-for crown of unwavering desires, the only prize thought worthy of being aspired to, was attained in the bright Jubilee spring of Rome.[2]

It marks a blessed epoch in a life, to have had the grace of the priesthood superadded to the exuberant benedictions of the year. And it was not in usual course; it came of

1. The recollections of the period before the accession of Leo XII are contained in the separate Fisher Press volume in which Wiseman recalls the reign of Pius VII, his personal reminiscences of him, and of Rome in his times.
2. Wiseman became a student of the English College at its restoration in 1818 when he was sixteen. He was ordained priest on March 10, 1825.

lingering and lagging behind others. Every school-fellow had passed on, and was hard at his noble work at home; was gaining a crown in heaven, to which many have passed; and the loiterer was enjoying, simply enjoying, the fulness of that luxury, spiritual and intellectual, which he and they, so far, had only sipped.[1]

The life of the student in Rome should be one of unblend-ed enjoyment. If he loves his work, or, what is the same, if he throws himself conscientiously into it, it is sweetened to him as it can be nowhere else. His very relaxations become at once subsidiary to it, yet most delightfully recreative. His daily walks may be through the field of art; his resting-place in some seat of the Muses; his wanderings along the stream of time, bordered by precious monuments. He can never be alone; a thousand memories, a thousand associations accompany him, rise up at every step, bear him along.

There is no real loneliness in Rome, now any more than of old, when a thoughtful man could say that "he was never less alone than when alone." Where would one seek solitude more naturally than in the very cemetery of a cemetery, where the tombs themselves are buried, where the sepulchres are themselves things decayed and moulder-ing in rottenness. Now in Rome such places exist, yet are peopled still, thronged as streets elsewhere are.

That heap of mould contains as yet a whole family, many generations of it, the Nasones, for instance, to which Ovid belonged, or an entire tribe, like the Freedmen, Liberti of Augustus; slaves gathered from all climates and moulded into one household, provided not only with board and lodg-ing in life, but also with cinerary accommodation after death, —with *amphorae* in the one, and with urns in the other,—or, one might say, with *ollae* in both. Or there, in

1. This is a reference to the fact that Wisemen undertook to read for a doctorate rather than taking priestly orders on the completion of his undergraduate studies and returning to England. He took his degree of Doctor of Divinity on July 7 1824 before his twenty-second birthday.

that labyrinth under-ground, still in a small space lie crowded the great band of noble Scipios, the founder of Rome's
transmarine empire, and preparers of her higher civilisation,
who thought it a glory to crown the sepulchral inscriptions
which recorded the highest titles of conquest abroad by the
bust of Ennius, the gentle father of poetry at home.

As Cicero was invited to hear them speak the wisest of
heathen morality, the kindliest whisperings of unhoping
consolation, so will they not allow us to be lonely whom a
higher law teaches to pity them, yet not to disdain to learn
from them. How easily, indeed, does the mind rise here to
higher thought. If these monuments show that the greatest
men considered it the greatest glory to have inscribed on
their sepulchral slabs, not the name of their own country
to distinguish them, but titles derived from distant regions
which they conquered; if Scipio cared more to be called
the Spanish or the African, than the Roman; and if, after
him, generals and emperors coveted the surnames of the
Parthic, the Germanic, or the British; what must be the
higher glory of him who not only absorbed all these titles
in himself, but crowned them all by that of the Empire
itself, which deemed invincincible, as it was, by those con-
querors, he subdued? Such was the Galilean fisherman,
who gained the title of "the Roman," the true "Pontifex
Maximus;" which title he has so transmitted to his successors, that "Roman Pontiff" and "Successor of Peter" have
become synonomous.

But to return: the student at Rome so peoples his
thoughts with persons, fills his memory with things seen
and heard, that his studies are, or ought to be, turgid with
the germs of life, rich as the tree in early spring in the
assurance of future bloom and fruit. On the darkest page of
abstruse theology there will shine a bright ray from an
object perhaps just discovered; but in the lighter one of
history and practical doctrine there literally sparkle beams
of every hue—like flowers reflected in a running stream—
from every monument and every record of the past there

present; so as to make it truly an illuminated page.

The very portrait of every heathen and every Christian emperor is distinct before the mind from numerous effigies; the Rome of his time is traced in ruins, sometimes in standing edifices; his actions are often written on arch or pillar; and many spots are signalised as having been the scenes of special occurrences connected with his reign.

Then the whole of Christian life and history—legible still, even to the traditional portraiture of apostles, martyrs and their Head, traced from catacomb to basilica and cloister—makes the history of the Church, her dogmas, practices, and vicissitudes, as vivid to the eye as any modern illustrated book can make a record of the past. Indeed, the monumental Church history, by the learned Bianchini, in tables of each successive reign or age, is a volume well known to the learned, as compiled upon this principle.

If such be the student's enjoyment of Rome, exclusive of what art and other resources can supply, and indeed confined to the sphere of his own pursuits, what must be the golden opportunities of one who, freed from the yoke of repressive discipline, and left to follow the bent of his own inclinations, may plunge into the depths over the surface of which only he had been allowed to skim, and drink long draughts from the fountains which hitherto he could only taste? The recollection of them will come back, after many years, in images of long delicious strolls, in musing loneliness, through the deserted ways of the ancient city; of climbing among the hills, over ruins, to reach some vantage-ground for mapping the subjacent territory, and looking beyond on the glorious chains of greater and lesser mountains, clad in their imperial hues of gold and purple; and then perhaps of solemn entrance into the cool solitude of an open basilica, where your thought now rests,—as your body then did, after the silent evening prayer,—and brings forward from many remembered nooks, every local inscription, every lovely monument of art; the characteristic feature of each, or the great names with which it is associated.

The Liberian speaks to you of Bethlehem and its treasured mysteries;[1] the Sessorian of Calvary and its touching
relics.[2] Baronius gives you his injunctions on Christian
architecture inscribed, as a legacy, in his title of Fasciola;[3]
St Dominic lives, in the fresh paintings of a faithful disciple,[4] on the walls of the opposite church of St Xystus;
there stands the chair, and there hangs the hat of St
Charles,[5] as if he had just left his own church, from which
he calls himself, in his signature to letters, "the Cardinal of
St. Praxedes;" near it, in a sister church, is fresh the memory of St Justin Martyr,[6] addressing his Apologies for

1. Santa Maria Maggiore, also known as the Liberian, has the relics of the Lord's
Crib at Bethlehem beneath the High Altar: it is here the Pope celebrated Midnight Mass at Christmas—hence Wiseman's reference to Bethlehem.
2. The Sessorian Basilica is the Basilica of S Croce in Gerusalemme,
built on the site of the Sessoran Palace, the residence of St Helena, the
mother of Constantine the Great, in Rome. This Basilica contains a
relic of the True Cross, and other relics associated with the Passion—
hence Wiseman's reference to Calvary.
3. Cardinal Cesare Baronius was a disciple of St Philip Neri and author
of the "Annales." He was Cardinal of Ss Nereus and Archilleus (the
"Titulus of Fasciola"). Baronius had the church reordered according to
Rennaissance ideas of what early Christian architecture ought to look
like. This explains Wiseman's comment about "injunctions in Christian
architecture." It was reportedly given to Baronius by the Pope as a sort of
joke because Nereus sounded like Neri. The Church is still in the care of
the Oratorians. Its frescoes are by Il Pomerancio, who also painted the
English Martyrs on the walls of the English College.
4. Père Besson.
5. St Charles Borromeo as a reforming bishop was instrumental in
putting into effect many of the Decrees of the Council of Trent in his
diocese. His influence on the Counter-reformation is comparable with
that of St. Ignatius Loyola and St Philip Neri. His titular church in
Rome was St Xystus. He was canonised in 1610.
6. St Justin (c.100-165), was born at Nablus in Samaria of Greek parent-
age. Educated in rhetoric, poetry, history and philosophy at Ephesus and
Alexandria, he became a Christian c.130, Commonly regarded as the first
Christian philosopher he held disputations with Jews, pagans and Christian heretics. The authentic record of his trial during the imperial rule of

Christianity to heathen emperor and senate, and of Pudens and his British spouse;[1] and, far beyond the city gates, the cheerful Philip is seen kneeling in St Sebastian's, waiting for the door to the Platonia to be opened for him, that he may watch the night through, in the martyrs' dormitory.[2]

Thus does Rome sink deep and deeper into the soul, like the dew, of which every separate drop is soft and weightless, but which still finds its way to the root of everything beneath the soil, imparting there, to every future plant, its own warm tint, its own balmy fragrance, and its own ever rejuvenescent vigour. But this is only its outward life. It would be difficult to describe what may be learned by one who will search its inward being, its innumerable reposi- taries of art, its countless institutions of charity, its private, as well a public, resources for mental culture, in libraries, in

Marcus Aurelius has survived. He was put to death in Rome after refusing to sacrifice to the gods in 165BC.

1. The sister church of St Pudentia, Wiseman's own titular church, was on a site which had belonged to Pudens, a Roman senator and friend of the poet Martial. Puden's wife, Claudia, was British. Tradition has long identified Pudens and Claudia as the couple mentioned in St Paul's Sec- ond Letter to Timothy (Timothy 4:21) as parents of Praxedes and Pudentiana both of whom have ancient Roman churches dedicated to them.

In his Epigram in Book XL. LIII Martial praises Claudia as follows:

> Claudia caeruleis cum sit Rufina Britannis
> > edita, quam Latiae pectora gentis habet!
> quale decus formae! Romanum credere matres
> > Italides possunt. Atthidses esse suum.

[Although Claudia Rufina comes from the race of the woad-stained British, how like those of a Latin are her feelings and graceful figure: mothers of Italy could take her for a Roman, and those of Attica for one of their own.

2. The Platonia is a underground chapel behind the apse of the Church of St Sebastian; the site of the chapel is where the bodies of Ss Peter and Paul were temporarily deposited in a catacomb during a persecution ("the martyrs' dormitory"), as Pope St. Damasus records in a metric inscription.

museums, in academies, in associations for every object, through the discussion, bi-weekly, of theological themes, to the hebdomadal dissection of a line of Dante.[1] Who has remained in Rome for his intellectual cultivation, and does not remember the quiet hours in one of the great public libraries, where noiseless monks brought him, and piled around him, the folios which he required; and he sat as still amidst a hundred readers as though he had been alone?

But there is an inner apartment in this great house; and he who may have penetrated into it, the very *penetrale*, will look back upon the time with pleasurable regret. Imagine him seated alone in the second hall of the Vatican library, round which are ranged now empty desks—for it is vacation time;—while above there is a row of portraits of eminent librarians, many distinguished for the learning more than for the purple. A door opposite gives a view of the grand double hall beyond, divided by piers. The cases round them and along the walls are the very treasure shrines of learning, containing only gems of manuscript lore. Above, all is glowing with gold and ultramarine, as airy and brilliant as the Zuccari[2] could lay them. The half-closed shutters and drawn curtains impart a drowsy atmosphere to the delicious coolness, which gives no idea of the broiling sun glaring on the square without. Imagine, however, no idler—for such a one could not gain access there at such a season,—but an assiduously plodding, perhaps dull-looking emaciated student, in whose hand crackles the parchment of some old dingy volume, whose turn has come of the many around him, to be what is called collated, a verb that has no connection with its analogous substantive. Perhaps, at the moment of a delightful discovery;—that the dusky membranaceous document has, in a

1. Wiseman remarks: "There used to be, perhaps there still is, a select literary society, meeting weekly to read papers exclusively on Dante."
2. The brothers, Tadeo (1529-66) and Frederico (1543-1609) Zuccaro produced frescoes in the Mannerist style for some of the Vatican rooms.

certain spot, a preposition or even a letter different from three companions;—there enters silently a man of middle age, with lofty brow, and deep-set eyes, happy in the loose drapery of home in summer—for he lives among books—and sits down beside the solitary learner. Kind and encouraging words, useful practical information, perhaps a discussion of some interesting point, made a quarter of an hour's diversion from the "weight of the day and the heat;" but—coming from or shared with the discoverer of Cicero and Fronto, of Isocrates and Dionysius[1]—they may become the beginning of a long-cherished and valued friendship. Hours like these, often repeated, pass not away lightly from the memory. Spent under the very shadow of the great dome, they endear Rome by the recollection of solid profit thus gained, and garnered for the evil days of busier life. Anyone, surely, whose years of mental cultivation can thus associate themselves, must retain a happy and grateful impression on mind and heart.

Thus far, the chapter has been very rambling, and possibly it will continue somewhat of the same character. The difficulty, in fact, of the present task increases most sensibly at this point, where arise personal contacts and more familiar intercourse with those of whom we treat; and where a hitherto distant and reverential acquaintance with their qualities matures into close observation, actual experience, and sensible enjoyment. The circumstances under which those qualities were learned and felt come so thoroughly home to their recorder, that he must shrink from the undue

1. The scholar alluded to here is Angelo Mai who was born in Bergamo in 1782. He entered the Society of Jesus and because of his scholarly ability he was put in charge of the Ambrosian Library in Milan. He moved to Rome in 1819 where he discovered in the Vatican Library many lost classical works including Cicero's *De Republica*, the Letters of Fronto, and those of the Emperors Marcus Aurelius and Lucius Verus, as well as works of Isocrates and Dionysius. In due course he succeeded Cardinal Lambruschini as Chief Vatican Librarian. He was created a Cardinal in 1840. See also Wiseman's *Pius VII* pp.54-5.

prominence into which he is obliged to thrust himself to
give them reality; and hence there is no alternative but that
of suppressing what would be most life-like, because most
confidential.

To explain this, it may be briefly stated, that this short
Pontificate formed the decisive era in the writer's life, that
pivot on which its future, long or short, was to turn. Every
one has such a date to look back upon; so there is nothing
wonderful in this. It merely happened in the writer's case
that, having finished his studies at an early period, he was
found to be at hand in 1826, when some one was wanted
for the office of Vice-Rector, and so was named to it. And
in 1828, when the truly worthy Rector, Dr. Gradwell, was
appointed Bishop, he was, by almost natural sequence,
named to succeed him.

These official positions necessarily gave rise to more frequent opportunites, and an occasional obligation, of
approaching the Sovereign. For in Rome such access is easy,
and almost indispensable for persons holding an ecclesiastical situation of responsibility. And in the instance alluded
to, there is attached to the headship of the college an
agency of English ecclesiastical affairs, which, though mainly conducted through ministerial channels, involves from
time to time good reason for addressing the Pope in person.
As a general recollection of these frequent audiences, it
may be simply stated, that they were uniformly condecend-
ing, fatherly, and most amiably conducted in look and
speech. It required some restraint on oneself not to be too
familiar. However insignificant the occasion or the person,
there was always the same benignant interest shown, as if
both had been invested with a much higher character.

Let us take a trivial example; one alluded to in our second
chapter. A student has reached the conclusion of his studies,
and is thought by his superiors—for it can never be a matter
of personal choice—able to claim his degree by public chal-
lenge against all comers who dare impugn any of his
propositions. To the honour of the English College be it

said, that, from time to time, one or other of its sons has hung up his shield, and stood bravely against his adversaries.

Let us take for an example one of these; and probably to many readers of this sketchy narrative an account of the proceedings may be new. The youth selected will have the ordinary power of application and memory, will not be too bashful or timid, must possess a fair amount of tact, and a readiness, if possible a fluency, in the use of the Latin language, not merely in its classical construction, but also in its scholastic and more barbaric technologies. He prints in a goodly quarto his thesis, which must contain fewer than a hundred points, but which probably his professors may carry up to four times that number, embracing the entire field of Catholic theology. This little volume is circulated among friends, and an invitation is sent to every ecclesiastical establishment in Rome; day and hour and place being specified, with the usual clauses, that in the morning "*datur omnibus*," all may attack; while in the afternoon the same liberty is granted only after three well-selected champions shall have broken their lances.

When the time comes, the respondent finds himself, he hardly knows how, seated behind a table at the end of an immense hall, which it requires a sustained voice to fill, supported by his professors, who may edge in a word at his ear in case of possible straits. A huge oval chain of chairs stretches down the room, on either side, and soon begins to be occupied by professors, doctors, and learned men, of whom he has heard perhaps only in awe; each of whom receives a copy of the thesis, and cons it over, as if to find the weak point between the plates of mail, into which he will later try to thrust his spear. I remember well, in the particular instance before my eye, that a monk clothed in white glided in and sat down in the inner circle; but though a special messenger was despatched to him by the professors, he shook his head, and declined to become an assailant. He had been sent to listen and report. It was F. Cappellari, who in less than six years was Pope Gregory XVI. Not far from him was seated the Abbé de la Mennais, whose works were so justly and so witheringly condemned. Probably it was the only time that they were ever seated together, when they thus listened to an English youth vindicating the faith, of which one would become the oracle, and the other the bitter foe.

Well, now some one rises, and in measured language, eloquently addresses a few encouraging sentences to his young competitor, whose heart is beating in anxious uncertainty on what side he will be assailed; till a period is rounded off, by the declaration of the number in his propositions about to be impugned. A crackling sound of stiff paper turning simultaneously in every hand through the hall filled with students, religious, and auditors lay and clerical, announces universal eagerness to see the selected theme, and relieves the tension of the pilloried youth, who, for the first time in his life, finds himself painfully conspicuous, and feels the weight of past labour and of future responsibility both pressing on his head.

Of course he has prepared himself thoroughly; and his wretchedness must be double, if he have left a vulnerable spot in his armour, or if it be not all proof. Of course he knows that no assaillant can "travel out of the record," or put such questions to him as St Thomas More did to the disputant "*in omni scibili et de quolibet ente*,"[1] whom he stumbled upon somewhere abroad, and thoroughly nonplussed by a most lucid query of English law; to wit, "*Utrum averia carucæ in vetito namio capta sint irreplegiabilia.*"[2]

Still there are subjects in which one is better got up than others; and there are some more interesting, more full of detail, and more suitable for a lively discussion. However there is no remedy; dryly or unctiously, logically or elo-

1. [On every possible topic of knowledge and whatever one might choose to ask.]
2. [Whether beasts for ploughing taken forfeit (in withernam) for a debt are able to be redeemed (replevied)]. Blackstone, iii.9.

quently, he must leave nothing unnoticed; he may turn the flank of something new, if it come unexpectedly before him; but, on the whole, he must show that he has overlooked no point worth answering.

The assailants are keen practiced gladiators, who, if they are satisfied of the defendant's prowess, will give him fair opportunity for its display. To this the writer must plead guilty; he has done his best to try the mettle of such young combattants striving to win their spurs. But when he has had such men as the Archbishop of Dublin or of Thyana,[1] or the Bishops of Pittsburg or Clifton, to attack, he has had no occasion to repent having well tempered his weapon, and weighted his blows.

After some hours of this digladiation comes a pause for reflection and repose, for every one but the champion of the day; who is probably crushed by a leaden sick-headache, in which his past performance looks a wretched failure, and his coming one a dark and dismal uncertainty. It arrives, however, and he is, this time, perched in a tall pulpit, with his professors low in front of him, hopelessly beyond reach for rescue and succour.

He is in the centre of one side of the nave of a lofty church, which not only adds solemnity and even religious awe to his position, but makes it necessary that his voice should ring clearly, in an almost declamatory tone, to reach the opposite side; where, on a dais, in a chair of state, sits the Cardinal who has accepted the dedication of the disputation.

It had been intended, in the case before us, to request the Sovereign Pontiff to bestow the honour of his patronage; but, at the last moment, this idea was abandoned. However, the inner circle was sufficiently formidable; one patriarch, four archbishops, at least half a dozen bishops, about twenty prelates, not a few of whom have since reached the highest honours of the Church, nearly as many professors, abbots, and rectors, and an immense crowd of persons of equal

1. Mgr. Barrili, subsequently Papal Nuncio to Madrid.

rank, out of full dress; which, being required in the inner circle, gives its appearance almost of a synod.[1]

Now, when this is over, what is the great reward looked forward to by the young athlete, beyond the titles of the theological doctorate obtained, but in Rome not borne? It is to proceed next day, with a suitably bound copy of the "Thesis," to the Sovereign Pontiff, and lay it at his feet. Not only does he receive a loving paternal blessing; but his cheeks glow and his heart beats as he bends beneath the expressions of the kindest encouragment, and even words of praise. He will find the common father of little as of great, already informed of the proceedings of yesterday, of any peculiar incident, some clever hit, some blundering obji- cient's courteous overthrow—whatever has been characteristic in manner or in method. And then he is exorted to persevere in study, and to cultivate to His glory the gifts which God has given him. Perhaps even more is said; a particular direction is pointed out, resulting from the success of the preliminary specimen; to study assiduously Holy Scripture, or the Fathers, or the questions of the day. All this used to be done by Leo, with a sweetness and emboldening graciousness, which would compensate to a youth any amount of labour undergone, for enrolment in such a prince's spiritual and theological army. It raised him

1. The above account is largely based on Wiseman's own Public Act at the Roman College for which he was awarded his Doctorate of Divinity before he had celebrated his twenty-second birthday. On 3 July 1823 Wiseman and his colleague Sharples went around in a carriage to dis- tribute copies of his thesis. On 7 July the first session was held in the saloon of the Roman College. He had to answer 12 objections and defend 400 propositions in all. The two masters were Piatti and Fornari. In the afternoon the session was in the Church presided over by Cardi- nal Zurla. The three objicients were Piccaroni, Del Signor and Padre Orioli. At the conclusion Wiseman took the oath and was awarded his Doctorate. Afterwards gelati were served.

On 11 July Wiseman gave a grand dinner for the three disputants and several Roman professors. (Wilfrid Ward: *The Life and Times of Cardinal Wiseman* Vol I, pp. 46-47).

above himself and his pusillanimous thoughts; made him, for the first time, hope that he might live to do some good; and opened his eyes to the brighter and more cheerful side of his own insignificant existence.

Such looks, such words, such a scene, are not easily forgotten; and who knows for how much sterling worth, and enduring work, the Church may be indebted to a single quarter of an hour thus bestowed on the tender, warm, and impressionable mind of a youth, accompanied by a benediction of grace, and proceeding from one whom he reveres and deeply honours, as God's very representative on earth? The seal is set and pressed deep upon the wax, just at the moment when it is the warmest and the softest; it would be wonderful if the impression were not sharp and lasting.

In the tempering of steel, after much manipulation, it is said that all the finest blades pass through the hands of one superior workman; who, by some secret skill and consummate tact, with a few strokes imparts a finish and delicacy that prepare them for the keenest edge. And so, after years of study and secret toil, a patient student may, in a few moments, receive what Milton calls "a touch of celestial temper," from the master-hand in the ecclesiastical armoury.

To have witnessed more than once such scenes has certainly left a strong impression, and confirmed all that has already been said in this volume, of the particular kindness with which Leo XII always treated those of our college who approached him, especially in connection with study. There will be further occasion to exemplify this assertion.

One demonstration of his interest in that establishment is little known. He had conceived a plan similar to that lately carried out by the present large-minded and munificent Pontiff, of extending the English College, and making it a place of prolonged education for students who might wish to attend the higher courses of the University. Annexed to the house is a large *Palazzo*, or residence let out into apartments, and built mainly by Cardinal Howard. The Pope commissioned Monsignor Nicholai, well known among the learned for a magnificent folio of St Paul's Basilica, and a very able practical work on the drainage of the Pontine marches which he had superintended, quietly to inspect these buildings, and ascertain the rent which they yielded, and the necessary outlay to be incurred by the proposed plan; also the funds requisite for an endowment, to carry it out permanently. For he desired that no loss should fall upon the college, but that rather it should reap complete advantage. However, death came prematurely to prevent the execution of these generous intentions, which were afterwards learned from Nicolai himself.

CHAPTER VI

CONTINUATION

THE instance of great interest and kindness alluded to, towards the close of the last chapter, was one which afforded the writer many opportunities of noting the undeviating goodness of heart which characterised this Pontiff. It so happened that a person connected with the English College was appointed to a chair in the Roman University.[1]

He had been encouraged by his professors to compete for it on its approaching vacancy. Having no claims of any sort, by interest or connection, he stood simply on the provision of the papal Bull, which threw open all professorships to competition. It was but a secondary and obscure lectureship at best, one concerning which it was supposed that few would busy themselves, or come forward as candidates. It was, therefore announced that this rule would be overlooked, and a person every way qualified, and of

1. There is little doubt that Wiseman is here referring to the competition which led to his own appointment as Professor of Oriental Languages at the University of Rome.

considerable reputation, would be named.

The more youthful aspirant unhesitatingly solicited an audience, at which I was present. He told the Pope frankly of his intentions, and of his earnest wish that the recent enactments of His Holiness should be carried out in his favour. Nothing could be more affable, more encouraging, than Leo's reply. He expressed his delight at seeing that his regulation was not a dead letter, and that it had animated his petitioner to exertion. He assured him that he should have a fair chance, "a clear stage and no favour," desiring him to leave the matter in his hands

Time wore on; and as the only alternative given in the Bull was proof, by publication of a work, of proficiency in the art or science that was to be taught, he quietly got up a volume through the press[1]—probably a very heavy one, but sprightliness or brilliancy was not a condition of the Bull. When a vacancy arrived, it was made known, together with the announcement that it had been filled up. All seemed lost except the honour of the Pontiff, to which alone lay any appeal.

Another audience was asked, and instantly granted, its motive being of course stated. I was again present, and shall not easily forget it. It was not necessary to restate the case. "I remember it all," the Pope said most kindly. "I have been surprised. I have sent for C—, through whom this has been done; I have ordered the appointment to be cancelled, and I have reproved him so sharply, that I believe that is the reason why he is laid up to-day with fever. You have acted fairly and boldly, and you shall not lose the fruits of your industry. I will keep my word, and the provisions of my constitution." With the utmost graciousness he accepted the volume, now treasured by its author, into whose hands the copy has returned, acknowledged the right to preference which it had established, and assured its author of fair play.

The Pope had, in fact, taken up earnestly the cause of his youthful appellant; instead of annoyance, he showed

1. *Horae Syriacae* 1827.

earnestness and kindness; and those who had passed over his pretensions with contempt were obliged to treat with him, and compromise with him on terms that satisfied all his desires. Another audience for thanskgiving was kindly accorded, and I witnessed the same gentle and fatherly temper, quietly cheerful, and the same earnest sympathy with the feelings of him whose cause had been so graciously carried through. If this young client gained no new energies, gathered no strength from such repeated proofs of interest and condescension, if these did not both direct and impel, steer and fill the sails of his little bark, through many troubled waters,—nay, if they did not tinge and savour his entire mental life, we may write that man soulless and incapable of any noble emotions.

The kindness, however, of Pope Leo XII for our national establishment was not confined to considerate acts towards individuals; but he gave all an unexpected proof of his singular condescension. I have already described the villa of the college,[1] where the vintage season is passed, half urban, half rural, unpretending in its size and accommodation, still more so in its architecture; for it is only a conglomeration of small houses. In fine, chiefly the view and position, in addition to the pleasant things done there, render it the very delight, the centre-point of affections, of every Roman student. Certes, if one who commands free choice wished to spend the day in that neighbourhood, there are stately villas and noble convents, all round the place, to tempt him to them.

Leo, still afflicted with many infirmities, never went far into the country. He had fitted up a small villa, what one might call, if not irreverent, "a box," three or four miles from Rome, whither he used to retire with his attendants, to pass a few hours in the vineyard that surrounds it. He had loved innocent sporting when a young man; and it used to be said that the quiet enjoyment of his old recreation was sometimes agreeable to him. Be that as it may, no

1. Wiseman's *Pius VII*, pp. 115-117.

recent Pontiff has been so sompletely a stay-at-home as he; and the papal villa at Castel Gandolfo was never, I believe, occupied by him. It could not, therefore, have been a mere love of excursion, or of locomotion, that would have drawn him into the Tusculum hills.

It was in the autumnal vacation of 1827, that certain preparations, of ominous import, attracted the attention of the students: loads of collegiate attire, furniture, and hangings arrived mysteriously, and were put aside; cleansing and painting commenced vigorously at a most inconvenient period; and then a supply, apparently superflous, of *gallinaceae,* cackling and gobbling arrived, no one knew whence, with a truly fatted calf from the great Borghese farm of Pantano, which, it was whispered, had been bespoken by an officer of the royal buttery. Rumours began to be afloat; yet no one dared to expect so unusual an honour as they bespoke for the little village. Only two persons were in the secret, The Rector and his Vice-rector, besides those engaged in the preparation. But secrecy was strictly enjoined and faithfully kept, till it was necessary to give orders for repairing the roads, cleansing the streets, erecting the triumphal arches, and hanging out tapestries; in which arts of adornment Italian villages are singularly expert. In fact, illuminations, fire-works, and a balloon, were added quickly to our preparations.

The culinary department was transferred from the ampler dispensations of the college cook to the more scientific operations of a courtly manipulator; and a banquet began to be prepared, the provider of which could no longer remain concealed. Yet, so strict were the precautions taken to observe secrecy, and prevent any concourse of people, that the highest officers of the household were kept in complete ignorance of the Pope's intentions. For, early on the 29th of October, there drove up to the house the Maggior-domo and Maestro di Camera (afterwards Cardinals Marazzani and Barberini), who asked why they had been sent thither? They had merely been told to drive in the morning to the Lateran gate, where they received a note directing them to proceed to the English villa at Monte Porzio. Great was their astonishment at learning that His Holiness was expected in a few hours. And, in like manner, we were under strict injunctions to admit no one into the house, invite no guest, as the visit was strictly to the college. Indeed, this the Pope again and again repeated, when deputations wished to approach him.

The morning was wet, and caused us much uneasiness, till, towards ten, the sun shone brighly, the clouds rolled away and every eye was intent on the road from Frascati, the Roman approach. Leaning over the garden wall, one saw into the deep valley along which it ran, now in long straight avenues, now diving and turning through dells, almost smothered in the vineyards, till the olive garden of the lordly but desolate palace of Mandragone cut short the view on earth and sky. Suddenly, at the farthest point of vision, some one declared that he had seen the gleam of helmet or of sword, through the elms, and was hardly believed; till another and another flashed on many straining eyes. Then the tramp of many horses, at full speed, was heard; and at long last along one of the level reaches of the road came into sight the whole *cortége*,—noble guards and dragoons galloping hard to keep up with the papal carriage and its six smoking sable steeds. Soon all was lost to eye and ear, as the cavalcade wound round and up the steep acclivity on which we were placed; then it rolled for a moment through the gateway of the village, and finally, after rattling through its narrow street, pulled up before the house. The Pope alighted, gave his blessing to all around him then walked to the public church, and made his prayer of adoration. He thence proceeded on foot to a neat house in the little square, from the balcony of which he blessed the assembled inhabitants; and where he received most affably the more respectable villagers.

After this, we had him all to ourselves: for dinner-time soon arrived. By strictest etiquette, the Sovereign Pontiff never has anyone to dine with him in his palace. Not even

a Sovereign is ever admitted there to hospitality. During
the genial month of October, there is so far a relaxation
from this rule, that entertainments are given by the Pope
out of the papal apartments, sometimes in an elegant pavil-
lion in the Vatican garden; and during that season of the
year the Pope visits monasteries or other institutions out of
Rome, where on account of distance, a repast is prepared
for him, of which the intimates partake. But, even so, the
rule is observed of his dining alone. A small table is placed
at the head of the guests' table, raised just perceptibly above
its level, by means of a low step, at which he sits alone,
though scarcely removed from the rest of the party.[1]

It was thus that Leo XII was situated, on the memorable
day of his visit to Monte Porzio. The table was laid for him
with elegance and simplicity; there was no display, no plate,
no attempt to be more than things and persons were. We
were in a college refectory, we were simple English superiors
and students. The rest of the table was covered with the
plain requisites for the meat and drink which supplied our
ordinary repast. The refectory was a low oblong room, at
the end of which, opposite the Pope, a large window
opened to the ground, and was filled up, as though it had
been a glowing picture, by a green and sloping mountain,
with vineyard below, chestnut and cypress above, and rich
green pasture joining them to the azurest of skies. The first

1. A short while ago, when the Pope was at Florence, the English Minister left it, and returned home suddenly. There was sufficient obvious
reason for this in the serious illness of a brother, whose dying hours he
was summoned to attend. This, however, was not a satisfactory reason for
a newspaper correspondent, who assigned as the true motive, that our
envoy had been insulted by not being placed at the same table as the
Pope. Perhaps the custom mentioned in the text may explain the fact,
which the writer got hold of, and manufactured into one of those stories
supplied by such persons who throw discredit on the glorious progress of
the Pontiff through Italy. Both he and the Grand-Duke of Tuscany are as
incapable of offering a gratuitous insult to a foreign envoy, as Lord N. is
of considering himself insulted by the observance of established court
rules. At any rate, we have heard no more of this great diplomatic case.

observation that the Pope made was not a little flattering to his English guests. "It is seldom," he said, " that a poor Pope can enjoy the pleasure of sitting down to dinner with such a fine set of young men." And truly the party did no dishonour, either by complexion, by stature, or by sinewy build, to the bracing air which they first breathed on earth. How are they now scattered, above the earth and beneath it! Several worthily fill episcopal chairs; many are labouring, with meritorious industry, in the ecclesiastical field; a large proportion have reached their hour of rest. However, on that day all were blithe and happy, joyful and jocund, under their Father's smile and kindly looks.

For the Pope ate scarcely anything, and barely tasted drink. But he would employ his leisure in carving, and sending down dishes from his own table; while his conversation was familiar, and addressed to all. He told us how he spent his day, partly by way of apology for seeming to partake so sparingly of the fare before him. He rose very early, perhaps at five; and spent the first part of the day, as any Catholic ecclesiastic does, in those religious duties which have to consecrate his actions,—meditation, prayer, and the celebration of the Divine mysteries, followed always, in the Pope's diary, by assisting at a second mass "of thanksgiving," said by a chaplain. A cup of coffee, or a basin of broth, with no solid food, was all the sustenance which he took till his hour of dinner. He went though the morning work of audiences, from eight, at latest, till twelve; then retired for private occupation, rested, devoted an hour to prayer (as we learned from others), drove out, and resumed public business till ten, when he took his first and only meal. To say that it was frugal would be little; nor could we wonder at the accredited report that he would not allow his personal expense to exceed a dollar a day, when we heard from his own lips that the dry Newfoundland stock-fish, the *baccalà* of Italy, was his very ordinary and favourite food.

This abstemiousness enabled Leo to go through functions which no other Pope in modern times has attempted, such as singing mass at Santa Maria Maggiore on Christmas Eve, which involved fasting from the previous midnight—at least three and twenty hours; then going to St. Anastasia's Church, the "Station" for the mass at dawn; after saying which, he sang the third mass at St Peters on the day itself.

To proceed, however; after our cheerful meal, the Pope retired into the Rector's bedroom, where he reposed for a short time; then he came into his modest sitting-room, where we again gathered around him, in familiar conversation, till the hour of his departure. He would not sit on the gold and damask chair prepared for him, but took possession of an ordinary one, with a rush seat, where he gave audience also to the good clergy of the village, able though plain, and certainly most disinterested, men; who, living chiefly on their own patrimonies, performed well the subsidiary duties which a solitary rector could not have adequately fulfilled. I remember well the questions which he asked, and some peculiar advice which he gave of a quite local nature.

The simple events of that day may appear trifling to many readers, who are accustomed to look upon the Pope as only an object of a peculiar class of feelings veering between the bitter and the sour. They forget that he is, at any rate, a sovereign; and one may presume that, if there existed an English "educational establishment" connected with Protestantism in even a small state, such as Baden or Sardinia, and the ruler of that state were to go and give the boys a day to themselves, dining in their hall, it would be considered a very gracious act, and perhaps a national compliment; at least a mark of respect for the people to which it belonged. The ecclesiastical Sovereign of Rome, too, is considered, popularly, as living in almost inaccessible state, and not easily drawn into familiar contact with others. Surely, then, it is no wonder that such an act of condescension endeared Leo to those who experienced it, unasked from him;—foreigners though they were, and of a nation which had shown little of that sympathy with him which it had lavished on his predecessor. But to their eyes such a visit was much more than one from a lesser sovereign. His ecclesiastical elevation, his spiritual principality, his religious character, render his worldly position only secondary, and give him a precedence in the hierarchy of monarchs, which the possessors of wider territories and of heavier budgets will not deny. An act of paternal condescension from one so considered, such as has been described, could not fail to remain engraven on the hearts of all who witnessed it, or rather experienced it. They wished their successors also to keep it before their minds; and therefore had the memory of this kindness graven upon something less perishable than those fleshy tablets;—upon two handsome marble slabs, one in the college, and one in the hall so highly honoured, varying only in the designation of place. The following is a copy of the first:—

HONORI

LEONIS · XII PONT.· MAX.

OPTIMI · ET · INDVLGENTISSIMI · PRINCIPIS

QVOD · IV. KAL. NOV. AN. MDCCCXXVII

ALVMNOS · COLLEGII · ANGLORVM

PORTIODVNI · RVSTICANTES

LIBENS · INVISERIT

IN · CONVIVM · ADHIBVERIT

OMNIQVE · COMITATE · COMPLEXVS · SIT

ROBERTVS · GRADWELL · RECTOR · COLLEGII

ET · IIDEM · ALVMNI

V.E. FLACIDO · ZVRLA · CARD. PATRONO · SVFFRAGANTE

DEVOTI · GRATIQVE · ANIMI · MONVMENTVM

DEDICAVERVNT[1]

1. [For the honour of Pope Leo XII, the finest and most sympathetic of sovereigns. On the 29 October 1827 he visited the students of the English College when they were at their country retreat at Monte Porzio, dined in their company, and was received most affectionately. With the support of the College's patron his Eminence Cardinal Zurla, the Rector of the College, Robert Gradwell, and the students, have dedicated this memorial tablet recording the visit of a devout and graceful spirit.]

CHAPTER VII

THE ENGLISH CARDINALATE

ALTHOUGH it was his successor Pius VIII who first, in
modern times created an English Cardinal, the idea of
doing so arose in the mind of Leo XII under circumstances
of a peculiar nature. It is a common practice for a cardinal,
on being raised to the pontifical chair, to "restore the hat,"
as it is called, by raising to the dignity, from which he has
himself just risen, some member of the family of the Pope
who had elevated him to that honour. And if that Pontiff
had belonged to a religious body, it would be, or might be,
restored to his order.

Now Leo XII had been created a Cardinal by Pius VII,
who was a member of the Benedictine order; and he wished
to discharge his duty of gratitude towards that venerable
corporation. In the winter of 1826 there arrived in Rome
the Right Reverend Dr Baines, Bishop of Siga, and Coadjutor of the Western District. He came in a state of almost
hopeless illness, with an interior abscess working on an
enfeebled frame and constitution, apparently unable to
expel it from the system. He came merely as a visitor, with
some private friends who had kindly accompanied him, in
hopes that change of climate might do more than medicines or their administrators. They were not deceived. The
mild climate, the interesting recreation, and perhaps, more
still, the rest from labour and excitement in which he had
lived, did their duty; at some due period, the interior enemy
capitulated, in that Englishman's stronghold of misery and
pain—the liver; and a visible change for the better was
observed by spring. A delightful summer spent between

Assisi and Porto di Fermo completed the task; and he used to recount, on his return, the astonishment of the simple rustics among whom he lived, at receiving payments by a strip of paper, with a few lines upon it—as illegible to them as a doctor's prescription is to more educated people—which, upon being presented at a certain palazzo in the neighbourhood city, they found, to their amazement, unhestatingly converted into the exact amount due to them, in clearly ringing coin.

By degrees the reputation which he had acquired in England began to spread in Rome; several noble families in which he had been intimate at home were in Rome, and gave many others the opportunity of becoming acquainted with him; and he had a power of fascinating all who approached him, in spite of a decided tone and manner which made it difficult to differ from him in opinion. He had sometimes original views upon a certain class of subjects; but on every topic he had a command of language, and a clear manner of expressing his sentiments, which commanded attention, and generally won assent. Hence his acquaintances were always willing listeners, and soon became sincere admirers, then warm partisans.

Unfortunately this proved to be a dangerous gift. When he undertook great and magnificent works, he would stand alone: assent to his plans was a condition of being near him; anyone who did not agree, or who ventured to suggest deliberation, or provoke discussion, was easily put aside; he isolated himself with his own genius; he had no counsellor but himself; and he who had, at one time, surrounded himself with men of learning, of prudence, and of devotedness to him, found himself at last almost alone, and fretted a noble heart to a solitary death.

At the period, however, to which this chapter belongs, these faults could scarcely show themselves to any great disparagement of his higher and better powers. In the course of the ensuing winter he was able, though contrary to the opinion of his friends, to appear in the English pulpit, which, as we shall see, Leo XII opened in Rome. The church, which was nearly empty when preachers of inferior mark occupied it, was crowded when Bishop Baines was announced as the orator. Many will remember him. He was happiest in his unwritten discourse. The flow of his words was easy and copious, his imagery was often very elegant, and his discourses were replete with thought and solid matter. But his great power was his delivery, in voice, in tone, in look, and gesture. His whole manner was full of pathos, sometimes more even than the matter justified; there was a peculiar tremulousness of voice, which gave his words more than double effect, notwithstanding the drawback of a provincial accent, and occasional dramatic pronunciations. In spite of such defects, he was considered, by all that heard him, one of the most eloquent and earnest preachers they had ever attended.

Such was the person destined, in the mind of Leo, to be the first English cardinal. The fact was, that Dr Baines was a Benedictine, brought up in the Abbey of Lambspring, and before his episcopal promotion Prior of Ampleforth in Yorkshire. We were informed by Monsignor Nicholai, that the Pope had called him, and said to him, "that he had been casting his eyes around him for a member of the Benedictine body, on whom to bestow the hat of restitution; many worthy men in it were too aged or infirm, others too young; so he had fixed upon the English monk, if, on enquiry, his character should prove equal to the proposed elevation." Such enquiries were made, in good measure amongst us, without their object being communicated. The result was, that the bishop was desired to remove from the private apartments in the Palazzo Costa, where he had been living with his English friends, to the Benedictine monastery of San Callisto, and to wear the episcopal habit of his order.

Pius VIII, I have been assured on good authority, renewed the offer, which the bishop now declined, and then only selected a very old Benedictine Abbot, Crescini, from Parma, to receive the hat which he, as well as Leo, owed to Pius VII. It was, indeed, given, but not enjoyed; for the good religious, who was quite worthy otherwise of his honours, died either on his journey, or immediately on his arrival at home.

It is evident, however, that Dr Baines would have been made a Cardinal, not on national grounds, but as a Benedictine. Still the thought of travelling so far to find a fitting member of that body for the dignity, was generous and broad in Leo. And besides, there can be no doubt that his intention was made the basis of the nomination of an English Cardinal in the ensuing Pontificate.

Gladly would this subject be ended here; it is not a matter of choice, but almost of necessity, to pursue it further. While it is a matter of absolute certainty, that Leo had made up his mind to name Bishop Baines a member of the cardinalitial college, had he ever turned his thoughts towards another of our countrymen, so far as outward manifestations can warrant us in saying so? Such an act would have exhibited nothing unreasonable in itself; though certainly the sudden creation of two English cardinals might have been unexpected. Leo XII was not the man to mind that; and if Dr Baines had been created as the representative of the Benedictine body, Dr Lingard might well have been so, on his own high merits, and as a reward for his splendid history.

Indeed, no one will venture to say, that in the whole range of modern literature, or in the annals of the British clergy, there is a name that could have been more worthily inscribed, or would have shone more brightly, on the roll of Roman dignitaries, than that of Lingard. An acquaintance begun with him under the disadvantage of ill-proportioned ages,—when the one was a man and the other a child,—had led me to love and respect him; early enough to leave many years after in which to test the first impressions of simpler emotions, and find them correctly directed, and mostly soundly based. Mr Lingard was vice-president of the college which I entered at eight years of age, and I have retained upon my memory the vivid recollection of specific acts of thoughtful and delicate kindness, which showed a tender heart mindful of his duties, amidst the harassing occupations just devolved on him, through the death of the president, and his own literary engagements; for he was reconducting his first great work through the press.[1] But though he went from college soon after, and I later left the country, and saw him not again for fifteen years, yet there grew up an understanding first, and by degrees a correspondence and an intimacy between us, which continued to the close of his life.

Personally, there was much kind encouragement in pursuits, and in views of public conduct; then—what is a more valuable evidence of regard—the mooting occasional points of difference for discussion, and from time to time "notes and queries" for information to be obtained, often formed the peculiar links of epistolary communication between us. Then, no one could approach him and not be charmed by the prevalent temperament of his mind. A boyancy, a playfulness, and a simplicity of mannner and conversation; an exquisite vein of satirical and critical humour, incapable of causing pain to any reasonable mind; a bending and pliant genius, which could adapt itself to every society, so as to become its idol, made him as much at home with the bar of the Northern Circuit, in the days of Brougham and Scarlett,[2] as with the young collegian who called to consult him at Hornby on some passage of Scripture or a classic. But a soundness of judgment and a high tone of feeling, united to solid and varied learning, strong faith, and sincere piety, supplied the concrete foundation on which rested those more elegant and varied external graces.

Such was Lingard to all who knew him, sure to be loved, if only known. Hence, though he never aspired to ecclesiastical

1. The Second Edition of Lingard's *The Antiquities of the Anglo-Saxon Church* was published in 1810.
2. The Bar honoured him by raising a subscription to present him with his own portrait.

honours at home, and his friends respected him too highly to thrust them upon him against his desire, it will never be known till his life is really written, and his correspondence published, how great a share he had in the direction of our ecclesiastical affairs in England, and how truly he was almost the oracle which our bishops consulted in matters of intricate or delicate importance. His works alone, however, will secure him his true place with posterity.[1]

That such a man should have received the highest hon-ours, should have been placed and stood on a level with a Mai or a Gerdil, a Baronius or a Norris, could not have astonished the literary or ecclesiastical world. It would have been *"plaudente orbe"* that he would have received his ele-vation. And it is most certainly true, that had mere merit always decided relative positions, he *ought* to have been what others were or are; but we must say of this lesser digni-ty what the gentle Metastasio makes one of his heroes, rather impertinently we must own, proclaim of the imperial state to his liege lord, not used to brook such sayings:

"......se

Regnasse sol chi è regnar capace,
Forse Arbace era Serse, e Serse Arbace."[2]

This, however, is not our question. Of Dr Lingard's deserts there is no second opinion. Nor is it at all necessary to throw doubts upon what is stated in the only meagre

1. The revival of interest in Lingard has been encouraged by the publi-cation of Edwin Jones' magisterial *John Lingard and the Pursuit of Historical Truth*, 2001, in which Jones argues that Lingard is the most important British historian since St. Bede.
2. Pietro Metastasio (1698-1782) was the most celebrated librettist of the 18th century. His work was set by Mozart, Gluck & Scarlatti. The quotation is from *Artaserse*, an opera composed for the Roman Carnival in 1730 by Leonardo Vinci to Metastasio's libretto. The quotation is from Act 1, Scene 1: "If only those reigned who were worthy to reign, then perhaps Arbace would have been Xerxes, and Xerxes, Arbace."

biography published of him, that Leo XII proposed to him
to settle in Rome, nor on the inductions drawn from the
conversation.[1] Of the first it is quite evidence enough, if Dr
Lingard wrote it himself to a friend. But, the question,
strange as it may sound, is really—"*Was* Dr Lingard actually
a cardinal?"

In the biography alluded to is the following passage:
"At the creation of cardinals in the following year, (Leo)
informed the Consistory that among those he had
reserved *in petto* for the same dignity was one, 'a man of
great talents, an accomplished scholar, whose writings,
drawn *ex authenticis fontibus*, had not only rendered great
service to religion,' but had delighted and astonished
Europe." In Rome this was generally understood to refer to
the historian of England.

When the Pope made this speech it must have been in
this form: "Moreover, *we create* a cardinal of the Holy
Roman Church, 'a man of great talents etc.,' whom, however, we reserve *in pectore*." He cannot reserve the creation of
a person, but only his promulgation; and this is so truly the
case, that if, ten years later, the Pontiff publishes a person as
a cardinal, declaring him to be the person so reserved, his
cardinalate dates from the first epoch, and he takes at once
precedence of all created in the interval. If, therefore, Dr
Lingard was the person meant by the Pope on the occasion
referred to in the foregoing extract, the English historian
was truly and really created a cardinal.

If so, what prevented his proclamation? The biography
goes on to say the Dr Lingard tooks steps to prevent it. Is
this possible? Is it consistent with his delicate modesty and

1. A conversation between the Pope and the historian related in
Fordyce's *History of the County Palatine of Durham* may be fairly put down
as legendary at best. Again, the Pope gives gold medals to many besides
cardinals. The present Pope follows this practice. He sent a gold medal to
Mrs Chisholm, to mark his sense of her great services to emigrants, and
three medals to Canova. On this subject also I can speak from experience; this mark of honour to Dr Lingard has no specific meaning.

sensitive abhorrence of praise even from a child, to imagine that he at once took to himself this description of a reserved cardinal? But the fact is, that such reservation is a matter of the strictest secresy, truly confined to the papal breast; not even the person who draws up the "allocution" has an inkling of it more than others, who can judge of the person by the qualities or actions attributed to him. These are often definite. The idea, however, of "Monsignor Testa," or any one else about the Pope presuming to decide whom he meant, and trying to "divert him from his purpose," is a simple impossibility. We may depend upon it that, if our historian was really created and reserved, he could not have got off thus easily. Either, therefore, the Pope changed his mind, or death prevented him from carrying out his intentions, though he lived more than two years afterwards; or, what was the fact, it was not to Dr Lingard that the Holy Father alluded. But "in Rome it was generally understood to refer to him." Here lies the mistake.

I well remember the day, the allocation, and its application. It was a noteworthy address when Leo emphatically intimated that in the creation of future cardinals he would not be guided by routine or court usages, but would select men of great gifts, and who had rendered signal services to the Church.[1] It breathed fully the spirit of Leo. At its conclusion came the mysterious reservation of a cardinal belonging to this highly qualified class. I well remember the excitement and delight with which our president, the old and affectionate friend of Dr Lingard, on coming home told us of the speech, saying, as from his own conjecture, that the characteristics assigned could possibly apply only to him. And so he repeated to others, friends of both, who, no doubt, assented, as we did, to his interpretation. But beyond

1. It as said that, on occasion of this declaration, a well-known cardinal, kind and good-natured, but whose career had been civil rather than ecclesiastical, and who had no pretensions to great acquirements in learning, turning to his neighbour, said, "It is as well that I am already a cardinal, or I should now stand no chance."

this circle, where Dr Lingard was known and appreciated, it certainly was not so; a very different person was then, and ever afterwards, and is still considered to have been the subject of the Pope's reservation.[1]

This was the celebrated Abbé de la Mennais.

As has been said, he had been to Rome in 1824, and had been received with the most marked distinction by the Pope. He was then in all the splendour of his genius, arrayed on the side not only of faith, but of the highest Roman principles. The boldness of his declarations on doctrine, the independence of his tone in politics, the brilliancy of his style, and the depth of thought which it clothed, put him at the head of religious champions in France. He had undauntedly assaulted the flying rear of the great revolution—the indifference which lingered still behind it, by his splendid *Traité sur l'Indifférence en Matière de Religion*; he had next endeavoured to beat back from reoccupying its place—what he considered had led to that

---

1. It is not natural to expect a writer, however great, to be much known out of his own country without translations. Now, indeed, many people learn foreign languages, and travel far from home; but, at the period in question, there were in Rome very few Italians who read English, or could translate it. Lingard's reputation was made abroad by his great *History of England*. His *Anglo-Saxon Church* and his *Tracts* had never been translated; and the version of his "History," made by Signor Gregori, was dragging its slow length along, through the hand-press, and through a heavy law-suit on the meaning of hot-pressing, till the translator's mental powers gave way, and the work was completed by the quicker and more eloquent pen of Signor (afterwards Father) Mazio. Till this was done the name of Lingard was known only to higher scholars. Take, for instance, the following extract from the Journal often quoted before:— "Aug. 3rd. 1921. Had private audience of the Pope. Presented petitions from Mr Lingard, Archer, and Fletcher, to be made Doctors. The Pope granted the petitions with pleasure. *I related several merits.* He told me to take the petitions to Mgr. Cristaldi, rector of Sapienza...I desired it might be done by complimentary briefs. The Pope assented. Dr. Gradwell was added to that number. He and Dr. Lingard received the degree of L.L.D. in additon to that of D.D.

fatal epoch and its desolating results,—a kingly Gallican-
ism. This he had done by a treatise less popular, indeed, but
full of historical research and clearness of reasoning: *La
Doctrine de l'Eglise sur l'Institution des Evêques.*

It was to this work that Pope Leo was considered to allude.
The text of the allocution in not accessible; but it was thought
to refer to this work with sufficient point. So matter-of-fact was
the book, so completely the fruit of reading and study, rather
than of genius and intellectual prowess, that it has been attributed to a worthy brother, who survives the more brilliant
meteor now passed away, in a steady and useful light. He is the
founder of an immense body of religious brethren, who have
their head-quarters at Ploërmel, but are scattered all through
Northern France, devoted to the education of the poor.

Be this as it may, the more celebrated brother has his
name on the title-page, and had well-nigh won its honours.
And then he was gathering round him an earnest band, not
only of admirers, but of followers, so long as he cleaved to
the truth. Never had the head of a religious school possessed so much of fascinating power to draw the genius,
energy, devotedness, and sincerity of ardent youth about
him; never did any one so well indoctrinate them with his
own principles as to make these principles invincible by
even his own powers. He was in this like Tertullian, who,
when sound of mind, "prescribed" medicines too potent for
the subtle poisons which he dealt out in his heterodox
insanity. Both laid their foundations too deep and made
them too strong, to be blasted even by their own mines.

How he did so mightily prevail on others it is hard to say.
He was truly in look and presence almost contemptible;
small, weakly, without pride of countenance or mastery of
eye, without any external grace; his tongue seemed to be
the organ by which, unaided, he gave marvellous utterance
to thoughts, clear, deep, and strong. Several times have I
held long conversations with him, at various intervals, and
he was always the same. With his head hung down, his
hands clasped before him, or gently moving in one another,

he poured out, in answer to a question, a stream of thought, flowing spontaneous and unrippled as a brook through a summer meadow. He at once seized the whole subject, divided it into heads, as symmetrically as Fléchier or Massillon; then took them one by one, enucleated each, and drew his conclusions. All this went on in a monotonous but soft tone, and was so unbroken, so unhesitating, and yet so polished and elegant, that, if you had closed your eyes, you might have easily fancied you were listening to the reading of a finished and elaborately corrected volume.

Then, everything was illustrated by happy imagery, so apt, so graphic, and so complete. I remember his once describing, in glowing colours, the future prospects of the Church. He had referred to prophecies of Scripture, and fulfilments of history, and had concluded that, not even at the period of Constantine, had perfect accomplishment of predictions and types been made; and that, therefore, a more glorious phase yet awaited the Church than any she had yet experienced. And this, he thought, could not be far off.

"And how," I asked, "do you think, or see, that the great and wonderful changes in her condition will be brought about?"

"I cannot see," he replied. "I feel myself like a man placed at one end of a long gallery, at the other extremity of which are brilliant lights, shedding their rays on objects there. I see paintings and sculpture, furniture and persons, clear and distinct; but of what is between me and them I see nothing, the whole interval is dark, and I cannot decribe what occupies the space. I can read the consequence, but not the working of the problem."

On another occasion his answer was more explicit. He had been discoursing eloquently on England, and what had to be done there in our religious struggles. He had described the ways in which prejudices had to be overcome, and public opinion won over. He was asked—

"But what, or where, are the instruments with which such difficult and great things have to be wrought?"

"They do not exist as yet," he answered. "You must begin

there by making the implements with which your work has
to be performed. It is what we are doing in France."

And glorious, indeed, were the weapons that came from
that armoury, of finest temper and brightest polish; true as
steel, well-balanced and without flaw, were the instruments
that issued from that forge: Montalembert, Rio, Cœur,
Lacordaire, Cornballot, and many others, who have not
failed in the work for which they had been destined by a
higher power than that of an earthly teacher.

But in de la Mennais there was long a canker deeply sunk.
There was a maggot in the very core of that beautiful fruit. It
was only in 1837, when he finshed his ecclesiastical career by
his *Affaires de Rome*, that the worm had fully writhed itself out,
and wound itself, like the serpent of Eden, round the rind. But
it had been there all along. During his last journey to Rome, to
which that book referred. he is said to have exclaimed to a
companion, setting his teeth, and pressing his hands to his
heart; "I feel in here an evil spirit, who will drag me one day to
perdition." That day soon came. It was the demon of pride and
disappointed ambition. Often has one heard good men say in
Rome, what a happy escape the Roman Church had experienced from one who had turned out so worthless! And others
have thought, that, if Leo's intentions had been carried out,
the evil spirit would have been exorcised, and, the dross being
thus removed, the gold alone would have remained. But
whenever was a passion cured by being humoured or satisfied?

It is easy to account for Leo's abandonment of his intentions in favour of this wretched man. But how nobly does
the character of our Lingard contrast with his, whom the
necessity of our task and topic has compelled us to consider
by his side! How sterling and manly, unselfish and consistent, does he appear throughout! For there can be no doubt
that, under assurance of its being made to him, he earnestly
recoiled from the offer of that high dignity, which no one
would accept without shrinking; though his mind might
balance between the examples of a Philip playfully rejecting, and a Baronius obediently receiving.

CHAPTER VIII

CLOSE OF LEO'S PONTIFICATE

THERE is an act of this papal reign which deserves record, as characteristic of the Pontiff himself, and as illustrating the practical working of the supremacy under complications otherwise insoluble. South America had thrown off Spanish rule, and enjoyed an independence of some years' duration. On the 21st of May, 1827, the Pope addressed the cardinals in Consistory assembled, on the ecclesiastical position of that continent. Spain had refused to recognise the independence of its many states, although it had ceased effectively to disturb them. It claimed still its old rights over them; and, among them, that of episcopal presentation. The exercise of such a power, if it existed, would have been contradictory to its object, and therefore self-defeating. Bishops are intended to feed a flock; and of what use would bishops have been, who could never even look upon their sees or be heard by their people? For it would have been quite unreasonable to expect that the free republics would acknowledge the jurisdiction of the country which declared itself at war with them.

On the other hand, there had been no ecclesiastical treaty or concordat between these commonwealths and the Holy See, by which previous claims had been abrogated, and new rights vested in their present rulers. It was just a case for the exercise of the highest prerogative which both parties ackowledged to be inherent in the supremacy, however galling its application might be to one of them. In the allocution alluded to, the Pope announced, that, not feeling justified in longer permitting those sees to remain vacant, and those immense populations to wander like sheep without a shepherd, he had provided them with worthy pastors, without the intervention of either side, but in virtue of his supreme apostolic authority. The Court of Madrid was angry, and refused to admit the Papal Nuncio, Tiberi; and a little episode in the life of the present Pontiff arose from this passing coolness.[1]

The last recollection which shall be recorded of this good and amiable man may be considered too personal; but it relates to a public expression of his interest in our countrymen. On some occasion or other, it happened that the author accompanied the Rector to an audience of the Pope. This was in 1827. After transacting other business, His Holiness remarked, that there being no English Church in Rome, Catholics who came there had no opportunity of hearing the word of God, and even others who might desire to hear a sermon in their own language had no means of gratifying their wish. It was therefore, he said, his intention to have, during the winter, in some church well situated, a course of English sermons, to be delivered every Sunday. It was to be attended by all the colleges and religious communities that spoke our language. One difficulty remained; where was the popular preacher to be found? The Rec-

1. Pius VII, at the request of Cienfuegos, envoy of Chile, sent as envoy to that republic Mgr. Muzi, and as his assistant the Abbot Mastai, now Pius IX. Pius VII, dying before the expedition had sailed from Genoa, it was confirmed by Leo XII, who, in his brief, declares that Count Mastai had been orginally appointed by his desire, describing him as *"Nobis apprime clarus."* (one of our most distinguished). The commissioners sailed on October 11th, 1823, but were driven by stress of weather into Palma, the capital of Majorca. Upon ascertaining from their papers who were the ecclesiastics on board, and what their mission, the governor had them arrested, kept them four days in a common prison, subjected them to an ignominious examination in court, and was on the point of sending them to banishment in an African *presidio*, when common sense prevailed, and they were restored to liberty. See a full account in the *Dublin Review* vol. xxxiv, p. 469.

tor, justly approved the design, most unjustly pointed to his companion, and suggested him; though, with the exception of such juvenile essays as students blushingly deliver before their own companions, he had never addressed an audience.

However, the burthen was laid there and then, with peremptory kindness, by an authority that might not be gainsayed. And crushingly it pressed upon the shoulders: it would be impossible to describe the anxiety, pain, and trouble which this command cost for many years after. Nor would this be alluded to, were it not to illustrate what has been in my view through this volume,—how the most insignifcant life, temper, and mind may be moulded by the action of a great, and almost unconscious, power.

Leo could not see what has been the influence of his commission, in merely dragging from the commerce of the dead to that of the living, one who would gladly have confined his time to the former,—from books to men, from reading to speaking. Nothing but this would have done it. Yet, supposing that the province of one's life was to be active, and in contact with the world, and one's future duties were to be in a country and in times where the most bashful may be driven to plead for his religion or his flock, surely a command, over-riding all inclination, and forcing the will to undertake the best and only preparation for those tasks, may well be contemplated as a sacred impulse, and a timely direction to a mind that wanted both. Had it not come then, it never more could have come; other bents would have soon become stiffened and unpliant; and no second opportunity could have been opened, after others had satisfied the first demand. One may therefore feel grateful for the gracious severity of that day, and the more in proportion to what it cost; for what was then done was spared to one at a later period. The weary task to preacher and audience was lightened by the occasional appearance in the pulpit, before alluded to, of the eloquent Dr Baines, whose *copia fandi* (facility in speaking) and finished address prevented the total blight in its infancy, of the Pope's benevolent plan.

He made it, in fact, his own. He selected a church of most just proportions for the work, and of exquisite beauty, that of Gesù e Maria in the Corso; he had it furnished at his expense each Sunday; he ordered all charges for advertisements and other costs to be defrayed by the palace, or civil list; and, what was more useful and considerate than all, a detachment of his own choir attended, to introduce the service by its own peculiar music. Its able director, Canonico Baini, the closest approximator in modern times to Palestrina and Bai, composed a little motet with English words, for our special use. After this Pontificate the papal choir ceased to afford us help, and a falling off, no doubt, took place in this portion of our offices, except at times, as when we had the cooperation of a nobleman, then minister at Florence, whose music, under his own direction, was there heard by many with admiration.

An affectionate blessing, and a case containing a gold and silver medal, were a sufficient reward to the first preachers, at the close of Lent; but the Pope on Easter Eve sent to the college materials of a sumptious feast, of which, immediately on release from penitential discipline, a large and noble party of our countrymen partook.

Fatigued, and almost broken down by new anxious labour and insomnium, I started next day for Naples and Sicily; travelled around that island when it had yet only twelve miles of carriage road in it; ascended not only Vesuvius, but to the crater of Etna; encountered only trifling but charateristic adventures sufficient to amuse friends; and returned with renewed vigour home, to find our dear and venerable Rector appointed Bishop, and about to leave Rome for ever.

On the 6th of December, 1828, I received the last mark of kindness and confidence from our Holy Pontiff, in the nomination to the vacated office, and had subsequently my last audience of thanks, fatherly and encouraging as usual. On the table stood, as I had often noticed it, a paper-weight of marble with a silver lion upon it; which caught attention from the trifling circumstance that the back of the noble animal was saddled with several pairs of spectacles, no doubt of different powers. It became interestingly connected with what shortly ensued.

The Pope went through his Christmas duties, and even officiated on the 2nd of February, 1829, the Feast of the Purification, when a *Te Deum* is sung in thanksgiving for escape from the dreadful earthquake in 1703. But between the two festivals he had given intimations of a consciousness of his approaching end. He took leave of Monsignor Testa, his Secretary of Latin Briefs to Princes, at the last weekly audiences he had, saying, most affectionately: "A few days more, and we shall not meet again." He gave up the ring usually worn by the Pope to the custody of the Maggiordomo, or High Steward of the Household, telling him, as he hesitated to receive it, that he was its proper guardian, and that it might easily be lost in the confusion of an event which was shortly to ensue. But the most striking proof of presentiment was the following. Monsignor Gasperini, his Secretary of Latin Letters, went to his usual audience one evening. After despatching his business, Leo said to him, in his ordinary calm and affable manner: "I have a favour to ask of you, which I shall much value."

"Your Holiness has only to command me," was the reply.

"It is this," the Pope continued, placing before him a paper. "I have drawn up my epitaph, and I should be obliged to you to correct it, and put it into the proper style."

"I would rather have received any commission but that," said the sorrowful secretary, who was deeply attached to his master. "Your Holiness, however, is I trust in no hurry."

"Yes, my dear Gasperini, you must bring it with you next time."

It must be observed that in Italy, and particularly in Rome, much importance is attached to the peculiar purity of style in monumental inscriptions. The "lapidary" style as it is called (from the Italian word *lapide*, which means an inscribed or monumental tablet), is a peculiar branch of classical composition, confined to a few choice scholars. It differs from ordinary writing, not merely in the use of certain symbols, abbreviations, and set phrases, but much more in the selection of words, in their collocation, and in the absence of all rounded period and expletives; for which clearness, terseness, simplicity of construction, and the absence of a superflous phrase or word, must compensate. Some inscriptions lately proposed for public buildings in this country offend against every rule of the lapidary style; will sound ridiculous to foreign scholars, as they are almost unintelligible to natives; are long, intricate, and almost Teutonic, rather than Latin in construction.

> One half will not be understood,
> The other not be read.

Among those who were considered in Rome the most practically acquainted with the lapidary style was Monsignor Gasperini, first Professor of Belles-Lettres, then rector of the Roman Seminary, and finally Secretary of Latin Letters to the Pope. To this obliging, amiable and learned man many had recourse when they wanted an inscription composed or polished. He was the author of most put up in our college. At his next week's audience, he laid the corrected inscription before Leo, who read it, approved highly of it, thanked him most cordially, folded, and placed it under the lion-mounted slab, where it remained, till sought and found, a few days later, after his death. He transacted his business with his usual serenity; and, in dismissing him, thanked his secretary with an earnestness that struck him as peculiar. They never saw one another again upon earth.

On the 6th of February, after having decended by a private staircase to the apartments of the Secretary of State. Cardinal Bernetti, and held a long conference with him, he returned to his own closet, and resumed work. He was there seized with his last illness; and it was generally believed that an operation unskilfully performed had aggravated instead of relieving its symptoms. He bore the torturing pain of his disease with perfect patience, asked for the last rites of the Church, and expired, in calm and freedom from suffering, on the tenth.

He was buried temporarily in the sarcophagus which had enshrined for a time the remains of his predecessors, and then in a vault constructed in front of St Leo the Great's altar; where, in the centre of the pavement, corresponding by its lines with a small dome above, was inlaid in brass the following inscription, alluded to as composed by himself. No one can read it and fail to be touched by its elegant simplicity.

LEO . MAGNO
PATRONO . COELESTI
ME . SVPPLEX . COMMENDANS
HIC . APVD . SACROS . EIVS . CINERES
LOCVM . SEPVLTVRAE . ELEGI
LEO . XII
HVMILIS . CLIENS
HAEREDVM . TANTI . NOMINIS
MINIMVS[1]

1. [As a suppliant I commend myself to my patron Leo the Great. Here near his sacred remains I, Leo the Twelfth, have chosen to be buried. A humble dependant and the least of the Leos who bear so great a name.]

NICHOLAS WISEMAN

PIUS
THE EIGHTH

Fisher Press

PIUS THE EIGHTH

******

CHAPTER I

HIS ELECTION AND PREVIOUS HISTORY

A PONTIFICATE which commenced on the 31st of March, in 1829, and closed on the 1st of December of the following year, limited thus to a duration of twenty months, cannot be expected to afford very ample materials for either public records or personal recollections. Such was the brief sovereignty in Church and State of the learned and holy Pius VIII.

The election to this high dignity, and the succession to this venerable name, of Cardinal Francis Xavier Castiglione cannot be said to have taken Rome by surprise. At the preceding conclave of 1823 he was known to have united more suffrages than any of his colleagues, till the plenary number centred suddenly on Cardinal della Genga; nor had anything occurred since to disqualify him for similar favour, except the addition of some six years more to an age already sufficiently advanced. In fact the duration of the conclave was evidence of the facility with which the electors arrived at their conclusion. Leo XII died, as has been stated, on February the 10th. On the 23rd the cardinals entered the conclave; and fresh arrivals continued for several days. Indeed it was not till the third of March that Cardinal Albani, accredited representative of Austria in the conclave, and charged with the *veto* held by the Emperor, entered within the sacred precincts.

On the 31st of that month, he was the first to break through them, and from the usual place announce to the assembled crowds, that Cardinal Castiglioni was elected Pope and had taken the name of Pius VIII. It will be naturally asked, what were the qualities which secured to him this rapid nomination. His short pontificate did not allow time for the display of any extraordinary powers; nor would it be fair, without evidence of them, to attribute them to him. But there was all the moral assurance, which a previous life could give, of his possessing the gifts necessary to make him more than an ordinary man in his highest elevation.

In an hereditary monarchy, the successor to the throne may be known for many years to his future subjects, and he may have been, during the period, qualifying himself for his coming responsibility. He may have manifested symptoms of principles completely opposed to those of his father, or of his house; and given promises, or thrown out hints, of a total departure from domestic or hereditary policy. Or, he may have been a loose and abandoned crown-prince; a threat, rather than a promise, to the coming generation. Perhaps the young Prince Hal may turn out a respectable King Henry; or, more likely, Windsor Castle may continue, on a regal scale, the vices of Carlton House. The nation, however, rightly accepts the royal gift, and must be content.

For in compensation, the advantages of succession to a throne by descent are so great and so manifest, that the revival of an elective monarchy in Europe would be considered, by all who are not prepared to see it lapse into a presidency, as a return to times of anarchy and revolution. The quiet subsidence of an empire by election into one of succession, within our own days, proves that—even in a country which violent changes have affected less than they would have done any other—the best safeguards to peace and guarantees of order are most certainly found in the simple and instinctive method of transmitting royal prerogatives through royal blood. How much of Poland's calamities and present condition are due to perseverance in the elective principle!

But there is only one, and only one, necessary exception

to this rule. The sovereignty of the Church could not, under any circumstances, be handed down in a family succession; not even if it did not enforce the celibacy of its clergy. The head of the Church is not the spiritual ruler of one kingdom, and his office cannot be an heirloom, like crown-jewels. His headship extends over an entire world, spiritually indeed, yet sensibly and efficaceously: kingdoms and republics are equally comprised in it; and what belongs to so many must in fact be the property of none. At the same time it is evident that the duties of this sublime functional power, running through every problem of social polity, can only be discharged by a person of mature age and judgment: there could be no risk of regencies or tutorships, of imbecility or hereditary taints, of scandalous antecedents or present vices. Only an election, by men trained themselves in the preparatory studies and practices of the ecclesiastical state, of one whose life and conversation had passed before their eyes, could secure the appointment of a person duly endowed for so high an office.

They look, of course, primarily to the qualities desirable for this spiritual dignity. It is a Pope whom they have to elect for the ecclesiastical rule of the world, not the sovereign of a small territory. His secular dominion is the consequence, not the source, of his religious position. Certainly it cannot be doubted that in later times the electors have been faithful to their trust. What Ranke has shown of their predecessors is incontestable of more modern Pontiffs; that not only none has disgraced his position by unworthy conduct, but all have proved themselves equal to any emergency that has met them, and been distinguished by excellent and princely qualities.

That those characteristics which determine the choice of the electors do not first manifest themselves in conclave, but have been displayed through years of public life, in legations, in nunciatures, in bishoprics, or in office at home, must be obvious. Hence men of accurate observation may have noted them; and a certain indefinite feeling of anticipation may be general, about the probable successor to the vacant chair. In Cardinal Castiglioni many qualities of high standard had been long observed; such as could not fail to recommend him to the notice and preference of his colleagues. To say that his life had been irreproachable would be but little: it had been always edifying, and adorned with every ecclesiastical virtue.

Though born (November 20, 1761) of noble family, in the small city of Cingoli, he had come early to Rome to pursue his studies, and had distinguished himself in them so much, that in 1800, when only thirty-nine years old, he had been raised to the episcopal dignity in the See of Montalto near Ascoli. Here he had signalised himself by his apostolic zeal, and had consequently drawn upon his conduct the jealous eye of the French authorities. He was known to be staunch in his fidelity to the Sovereign Pontiff, and to the rights of the Church: consequently he was denounced as dangerous, and honoured by exile, first to Milan, and then to Mantua. We are told that those who had charge of him were astonished to find, in the supposed fire-brand, one of the gentlest and meekest of human beings. In all this, however, there was much to recommend him to those who had met to elect a shepherd, and not a hireling, for Christ's flock.

But in this proof of his constancy there had been testimony borne to another, and if not a higher, at least a rarer quality. This was ecclesiastical learning. Of his familiarity with other portions of this extensive literary field, there will be occasion to speak later. But the branch of theological lore in which Cardinal Castiglioni had been most conspicuous was Canon law. Some readers may not be willing to concede any great importance or dignity to such a proficiency, the value of which they may have had few opportunities of estimating. Canon law is, however, a system of ecclesiastical jurisprudence, as complex and as complete as any other legislative and judicial code: and since it is in force at Rome, and has to be referred to even in transactions with

other countries where ecclesiastical authority is more limited, a person solidly grounded in it, and practically versed in
its application, naturally possesses a valuable advantage in
the conduct of affairs, especially those belonging to the
highest spheres. We would not allow a foreigner the right to
despise that peculiar learning which we think qualifies a
lawyer of eminence for the woolsack; especially if from his
ignorance of our unique legal principles and practices, he
may not have qualified himself to judge of it.

However, the attainments of Cardinal Castiglioni rose
even higher than these. He had been orginally the scholar
of the first Canonist of his day, and had become his assistant. The work which stands highest among modern
manuals on ecclesiastical law is Devoti's Institutes: and this
was the joint work of that prelate and Castiglioni. Indeed,
the most learned portion of it, the notes which enrich and
explain it, were mainly the production of the pupil. Now it
so happened, that when the relations between Pius VII and
the French Emperor became intricate and unfriendly, and
delicate questions arose of conflicting claims and jurisdic-
tions, it was to the learned Bishop of Monalto that the
Pope had recourse, as his learned and trusty counsellor in
such dangerous matters. He was found equal to the occasion. His answers and reports were firm, precise, and
erudite; nor did he shrink from the responsibility of having
given them. It was this freedom and inflexibility which
drew upon him the dislike of the occupying power in Italy.
Surely such learning must possess its full value with those
who have seen its fruits, when they are deliberating about
providing a prudent steersman and a skilful captain for the
bark of Peter, still travailed by past tempests, and closely
threatened by fresh storms.

When the Pope was restored to his own, Castiglioni's
merits were fully acknowledged and rewarded. On the 8th
of March, 1816, he was raised to the cardinalitial dignity,
and named Bishop of Cesena, the Pope's own native city.
He was in course of time brought to Rome, and so became

Bishop of Tusculum, or Frascati, one of the episcopal titles in the Saced College. He was also named Penitentiary, an office requiring great experience and prudence.

He enjoyed the friendship of Consalvi as well as the confidence of their common master, and thus his ecclesiastical knowledge was brought most opportunely to assist the diplomatic experience and ability of the more secular minister. In fact, it might be said that they often worked in common, and even gave conjointly audience to foreign ministers, in matters of double interest. And such must often be the trasactions between the Holy See and Catholic Powers. Again, we may ask, was it not more than probable that such experience in ecclesiastical affairs of the very highest order, and such results of its application, should carry due weight with persons occupied in the selection of a ruler over the Church, who should not come new and raw into the active government of the whole religious world?

Such were the qualifications which induced the electors in conclave to unite their suffrages in the person of Cardinal Castiglioni; and it is not wonderful that he should have selected for his pontifical name, PIUS THE EIGHTH. Indeed, it has been said that the Holy Pontiff, to whom he thus recorded his gratitude, had long before given him this title. For, on some occasion when he was transacting business with him, Pius VII said to him with a smile, Your Holiness, Pius the Eighth, may one day settle this matter.[1]

Such auguries being seldom told till their fulfilment,—for without the modesty that would conceal them, there would not be the virtues that can deserve them,—they are naturally little heeded. To tell the truth, one does not see why, if a Jewish High Priest had the gift of prophesy for his year of office,[2] one of a much higher order and dignity should not occasionally be allowed to possess it. In this case the privilege was not necessary. As it has been already intimated, the accumulation of merits in the Cardinal might strike the

1. D'Artaud, *Life of Pius VIII*.   2. John xi.52.

Pope even more, from his closer observation, than they would the electors; and the good omen might only be the result of sagacity combined with affection. In like manner, a natural shrewdness which Pius possessed might have guided him to a similar prediction, if true as reported, to his immediate successor, Leo XII. It used to be said that when Monsignor della Genga was suddenly told to prepare for the nunciature, and consequentially for episcopal consecration, and was therefore overwhelmed with grief, he flew to the feet of Pius to entreat a respite, when the holy man said to him; "It is the white coif[1] that I put upon your head." The many noble gifts which showed themselves in the youthful prelate—sufficient to induce the Pope at once to send him abroad as his representative in troublesome and dangerous times—may have carried his penetrating eye beyond the successful fulfilment of that mission, to the accomplishment of one higher and more distant.

But it is more difficult to account for other auguries, where there can be no recourse to prophesy or shrewdness. All history is full of them: some we throw aside to the score of superstition, others we unhesitatingly give up to fiction; an immense amount we make over to what we call singular or happy coincidences; while a residue is allowed to remain unappropriated, as inexplicable or devoid of sufficient evidence to be judged on, as too slight to be believed, yet too good not to be repeated. In the earlier book, a little incidence was told of a coachman's good-natured omen to the young Benedictine monk, afterwards Pius VII, and the authority was given for it; only one removed from the august subject of the anecdote.[2] Another, and more strange one, recurs to mind, and rests upon exactly the same authority. I received it from the venerable Monsignor Testa, who assured me that he heard it from Pope Pius VII. Long before his elevation to the papacy the then Dom Gregory

1. The zucchetto, worn white only by the Pope.
2. *Pius VII*, by Nicholas Wiseman, p. 19 (Fisher Press , 2003)

Chiaramonti was a monk in Rome, and he often used to accompany his relation Cardinal Braschi in his evening drive. One afternoon, as they were just issuing from his palace, a man, apparently an artisan, without a coat and in his apron, leaped on the carriage step (which used then to be outside), put his head in the carriage, and said, pointing first to one and then to the other: *Ecco due papi, prima questo, e poi questo.*" "See two popes, first this and then this." He jumped down and disappeared. Had anyone else witnessed the scene from without, he might have been tempted to ask: "Are all things well? Why came this madman to you?" And the two astonished inmates of the carriage might have almost answered with Jehu: "Thus and thus did he speak to us; and he said, Thus saith the Lord, I have anointed you kings over Israel."[1] The Pope added that, after the fulfilment of the double prophesy, he had ordered every search and enquiry to be made after the man, but had not been able to find him. There had, however, been ample time for him to have finished a tolerably long life; for Braschi, as Pius VI, reigned nearly the years of St. Peter. [2]

1. IV Kings: 9: 11,12.
2. This anecdote brings to mind another concerning a very different person, which I do not remember to have seen published. A gentleman, who, though he differed materially in politics and in religion from the illustrious Daniel O'Connell, enjoyed much of his genial kindness, and greatly admired his private character, told me that he received the follwing account from him of his first great success at the Bar. He was retained as counsel in an action between the city of W——— and another party respecting a salmon weir on the river. The corporation claimed it as belonging to them; their opponents maintained it was an open fishery. Little was known of its history, further than that it was in the neighbourhood of an ancient Danish colony. But it had always been known by the name of "the lax weir," and this formed the chief ground of the legal resistance to the city's claim. Able counsel was urging it, while O'Connell, who had to reply for the city, was anxiously racking his fertile brains for a reply. But little relief came thence. Lax, it was argued, meant loose; and loosed was the opposite of reserved, or pre-

The new Pope chose for his secretary of state the Cardinal Albani, a man vigorous in mind, though advanced in years, whose views no doubt he knew to coincide with his own, and whose politics were of the school of his old colleague, Cardinal Consalvi. The house of Albani, too, was one of the most illustrious and noble in Italy, boasting even imperial alliances. In the Cardinal were centred its honours, its wealth, and what he greatly valued, the magnificent museum of which mention has before been made. He died in 1834, at the advanced age of eighty-four.

served, or guarded, or under any custody of a corporation. The point was turned every way, and put in every light, and looked brilliant and dazzling to audience, litigants, and counsel. The jury were pawing the ground, or rather shuffling their feet, in impatience for their verdict and their dinner; and the nictitating eye of the court, which had long ceased taking notes, was blinking a drowsy assent. Nothing could be plainer. *Lax* weir could not be a *close* weir (though such reasoning might not apply to corporation or constituencies); and no weir could have ever borne the title of lax, if it had ever been a close one. At this critical juncture some one threw across the table to O'Connell a little screwed up twist of paper, according to the wont of courts of justice. He opened, read it, and nodded grateful thanks. A change came over his countenance: the well-known O'Connell smile, half frolic, half sarcasm, played about his lips; he was quite at ease, and blandly waited the conclusion of his antagonist's speech. He rose to reply, with hardly a listener; by degrees the jury was motionless, the lack-lustre eye of the court regained its brightness; the opposing counsel stared in amazement and incredulity, and O'Connell's clients rubbed their hands in delight. What had he done? Merely repeated to the gentlemen of the jury the words of the little twist of paper. "Are you aware that in Danish *lachs* means salmon?" The reader may imagine with what wit and scorn the question was prepared, with what air of triumph it was put, and by what confident demolition of all the adversary's *lax* argumentation it was followed. Whether there was then at hand a Danish dictionary (a German one would have sufficed), or the judge reserved the point, I know not; but the confutation proved triumphant: O'Connell carried the day, was made standing counsel to the city of W————, and never after wanted a brief. But he sought in vain, after his speech, for his timely succourer: no one knew who had thrown the note; whoever it was he had disappeared, and O'Connell could never make out to whom he was indebted.

CHAPTER II

PERSONAL CHARACTER

THE appearance of Pius VIII was not, perhaps, so prepossessing at first sight as that of his two predessessors. This was not from any want either of character or of amiability in his features. When you came to look into his countenance, it was found to be what the reader will think it in his portrait, noble and gentle. The outlines were large and dignified in their proportions; and the mouth and eyes full of sweetness. But an obstinate and chronic herpetic affection in the neck kept his head turned and bowed down, imparted an awkwardness, or want of elegance, to his movements, and prevented his countenance being fully and favourably viewed. This, however, was not the worst; he seemed, and indeed was, in a state of constant pain, which produced an irritation that manifested itself sometimes in his tone and expression. One of his secretaries mentioned to me an instance: when, on his giving a good-natured reply, it immediately drew from the Pope the blandest of smiles, and a most condescending apology on account of his infirmities.

Another effect of this suffering was, that many of the functions of the Church were beyond his strength. For example, the *Miserere* in Holy Week, one of the most splendid of musical performances, from being exactly suited in its character to its circumstances, was obliged to be curtailed, because the Pope could not kneel so long as it required. This was indeed but a trifle; for, notwithstanding his constant pain, he was assiduous in his attention to business, and indefatigable in the discharge of every duty.

Being himself of a most delicate conscience, he was perhaps severe and stern in his principles, and in enforcing them. He was, for example, most scrupulous about any of his family taking advantage of his elevation to seek honours of high offices. On the very day of his election, he wrote to his nephews a letter in which he communicated to them the welcome news of his having been raised, by Divine Providence, to the Chair of Peter, and shed bitter tears over the responsibilities with which this dignity overburthened him. He solicited their prayers, commanded them to refrain from all pomp and pride, and added; "let none of you, or of the family, move from your posts." During his pontificate it was proposed to bestow on the great St Bernard the title of Doctor of the Universal Church, in the same manner as it is held by St Augustine or St Jerome. It was said that some one engaged in the causes, by way of enlisting the Pope's sympathies in it, remarked that St Bernard belonged to the same family; since the Chatillons from France and the Castiglioni in Italy were only different branches of the same illustrious house. This remark, however, whether in the pleadings or in conversation, sufficed to check the proceedings; as the Pontiff, jealous of any possible partiality or bias on his part, and fearful of even a suspicion of such a motive having influenced him, ordered them to be suspended. They were afterwards resumed, and brought to a happy conclusion under his pontificate.

In speaking of this Pope's literary accomplishments, his superior knowledge of Canon Law was singled out. But this was by no means his exclusive pursuit. To mention one of a totally different class, he possessed a very rare acquaintance with numismatics. His French biographer bears witness to his having held long conferences with him on this subject, which formed one of his favourite pursuits, while Castiglioni was yet a cardinal. He says that, when closeted with him for a long time, perhaps people in waiting imagined they were engaged in solemn diplomatic discussions, while, in truth, they were merely debating the genuineness or value of some Vespasian or Athenae.

Biblical literature, however, was his favourite pursuit; and the writer can bear witness to his having made himself fully acquainted with its modern theories, and especially with German rationalistic systems. Very soon after the Pope's accession, he obtained an audience, in company with the late most promising Professor Allemand, who occupied the Chair of Holy Scripture in the Roman Seminary, and had collected a most valuable library of modern bibilical works in many langauages. The Pope then gave formal audiences on his throne, and not in his private cabinet, so that a long conversation was more difficult. Still he detained us long, in which he encouraged his willing listeners to persevere, and gave evidence of his own extensive and minute acquaintance with their many branches. He had, however, supplied better proof of this knowledge than could be given in a mere conversation.

It is well known to every scholar, how thoroughly, for more than a generation, the Bible in Germany had been the sport of every fancy, and the theme for crude infidelity. The word "rationalism" gives the key to the system of stripping the sacred volume of the supernatural; explaining away whatever transcends the ordinary powers of nature or of man, whether in action or in knowledge, and reducing the book to the measure of a very interesting ancient Veda or Saga, and its personages to that of mythic characters, Hindoo or Scandinavian. Till Hengstenberg[1] appeared, most Protestant scriptural literature ran in the same channel, with more or less of subtlety or of grossness; now refined and now coarse, according to the tastes or characters of authors. More diluted in Michaelis[2] or Rosenmüller[3] the younger; more elegantly clothed in Gesenius;[4] more

1. Ernst Wilhelm Hengstenberg (1802-1869). Taught at the University of Berlin; defended the divine nature of the Christian religion and in particular the Protestant Augsburg Confession.
2. Johann Henry Michaelis (1668-1788), Professor of Divinity at Halle University.
3. Johann George Rosenmuller (1736-1815), Professor of Theology at Leipzig.
4. Frederick Henry Wilhelm Gesenius (1786-1842), Professor of Theology at Halle, celebrated Orientalist and author of a Hebrew Grammar.

ingenious in Eichorn,[1] and more daring in Paulus,[2] the same spirit tainted the whole of this branch of sacred literature from Semler[3] to Strauss[4], who gave the finishing stroke to the system, by the combination of all the characteristics of his predecessors, mingled with a matchless art that seems simplicity. Perhaps from this concentration of the poison of years arose the counteraction in the system or constitution of religious Germany, manifested by a return to a more positive theology.

This growing evil had manifested itself, up to a certain point only in Protestant divinity; and the universities of Heidelberg and Halle, Jena and Leipsig, were among the principal seats of this new infidelity. It was the more dangerous, because it had discarded all the buffoonery and mockery of the grinning *philosophe*, and worked out its infidelity like a problem, with all the calm and gravity of a philosopher. But at length there appeared a man whose works, professedly Catholic, were tainted with the neology of his countrymen, and threatened to infect his readers and his hearers with its creeping venom. This was Jahn,[5] professor of Scripture in the University of Vienna; a hard scholar, who used to say that no one need hope to push forward his art or science a step without studying eighteen hours a day; a really learned man, and of sound judgment, except on the

1. Johann George Eichorn (1752-1827), Professor at Jena and then at Gottingen; author of a History of Biblical Literature.

2. H.E.G. Paulus (1761-1851) proposed a theory of natural explanations of the miracles of scripture.

3. Johann Solomon Semler (1725-1791) was a celebrated Lutheran divine and Professor at Halle. In his *Historicae Ecclesiasticae selecta capita* he sought to explain away the miracles in the Holy Bible.

4. David Friedrich Strauss (1808-1874) studied and taught at Tubingen University. His life of Jesus of 1835 aimed to remove the supernatural entirely from the Gospels. George Eliot translated it into English in 1846. Strauss subsequently lost his faith and was buried without Christian ceremonies at his own request.

5. Johann Jahn (1750-1817) was obliged to vacate his chair of Oriental Literature at Vienna in 1806 because of his heterodoxy.

one point on which he so lamentably went astray.

He published two principal works, an introduction to the Old Testament, and a Biblical Archaeology: both most valuable for their erudition, but both dangerously tinged with the principles of infidelity, especially in the very principles of biblical science. These were both large works; so he published compendiums of them in Latin, each in one volume, for the use of students. But even into these the poison was transfused. Perhaps Jahn was soured and irritated by the treatment he received from his theological opponents, one in particular, immensely his inferior in learning, though sound in principle; and he certainly replied with acrimony and biting sarcasm. However, his works were justly prohibited, and in the end withdrawn from the schools.

It was a pity that they should be lost; and accordingly a remedy was proposed. This consisted of the republication of the two Introductions, cleansed of all their perilous stuff, and appearing under the name of a new author. This idea was either suggested, or immediately and warmly encouraged by Cardinal Castiglioni. The undertaking was committed to the learned Dr F. Ackermann, professor also at Vienna, and a friend of Dr Jahn's. The sheets of the volumes were forwarded to Rome and revised by the hand of the Cardinal. I cannot remember whether it was he who mentioned it himself at the audience alluded to, or whether I learned it from Dr Ackermann, with whom I then had the advantage of maintaining a profitable correspondence. His Commentary on the Minor Prophets proves the learning and ability of this excellent man to have been equal to much more than mere adaptions of the works of others.

But, at the same time, the part taken by Pius in this useful undertaking is evidence of his zeal, and of his accomplishments in the most essential branch of theological learning. Further evidence will not be wanting.

CHAPTER III

FRENCH AND ENGLISH CARDINALS

THE short duration of Pius's reign did not give opportunity for making any great addition to the Sacred College; nor indeed would this subject be considered of sufficient interest for general readers, were there not some peculiar circumsances here connected with it.

There is certainly no dignity in Europe more thoroughly European than the cardinalate; and there is no reason why it should not have, one day, its representatives in America, or Asia, or even Australia. It is indeed an ecclesiastical distinction, though admitted to possess civil rank throughout the Continent; but every other dignity is similarly confined to a particular class. A civilian cannot hope to be a general, or an admiral, or a lord-chancellor; nor can an ecclesiastic be in the House of Commons, nor can a lawyer obtain the Victoria Cross. Every honour has its narrow approach; every elevation its steep and solitary path. But each is limited to its own country. A Wellington may have a galaxy of stars twinkling in diamonds from the azure velvet of his pall; and a few crosses may be exchanged between allied nations. But there is no military power that flecks the uniform of the valiant—whether scarlet, blue or white—with a badge of honour; no "Republic of letters" which places laurel crowns on the brows of the learned and the scientific, in whatever-language they have recorded their lore; no bountiful Caliph, or Lord of Provence, to whom the gentle minstrel of every nation is a sacred being, entitled to good entertainment and respect. In fine, no secular power affects either to look abroad among foreign nations for persons whom to honour, as of right, or to expect other sovereigns and states to solicit for their subjects its peculiar badge of generally recognised dignity.

But the Church, being universal in her destinies, makes no national distinction, and the honours which she bestows are not confined to any country: but, on the contrary, they receive an acknowledgment, which in some may, indeed, be merely courteous, but in most is legally assured. The Code Napoleon, wherever it prevails, has this provision. As a matter of course, where there is good understanding between any government and the Holy See, the distribution of such a dignity is matter of mutual arrangement; and it must be the fault of the government if such amicable relations do not exist. There is consequently a recognised right in the four great Catholic powers, to propose a certain number of their ecclesiastical subjects for the cardinalitial dignity. Formerly when a general promotion, as it was called, took place, that is, when a number of particular persons holding certain high offices were simultaneously invested with the purple, the privileged Courts had a claim to propose their candidates. This usage may be considered almost obsolete; and indeed the reigning Pontiff has dealt most liberally in this respect, by naming more foreigners than ever before held place in that ecclesiastical senate.

To illustrate the different principles on which such an addition may be conducted, we may mention two of those whom Pius VIII invested with this high position, one French, the other English.

The first was of the noble family of Rohan-Chabot, which under the first of these designations belongs equally to Germany and to Bohemia, as a princely house; and in France traces descent from St Louis, and has infused its blood by marriage into the royal House of Valois. Its armorial motto has embodied in a few lines as strong a consciousness of all but regal claims, as such a distilled drop of family haughtiness could well enclose:

> Roi ne peux,
> Prince ne veux,

Rohan suis.[1]

No one could have a higher right by birth to aspire to the Roman purple, than had the Abbé Louis Francis Augustus, of the Dukes of Rohan-Chabot, Prince of Leon, who had embraced the ecclesiastical state. Moreover, he was distinguished by piety, sufficient learning, and unimpeachable conduct. In 1824, an effort was made to obtain for him the hat from Leo XII. The Pope replied, that France must be content to abide by its usage, of only proposing for this honour its archbishops and bishops. The French ambassador, whose relation the young Duke was, made every exertion for him; but when, in his absence his *chargé d'affaires*, in an audience, proposed the subject, the Pope, in his sweetest manner, replied by a Latin verse,

Sunt animus, pietas, virtus; sed deficit aetas.[2]

The applicant was rather surprised at this ready and complete reply, which did full justice to both sides of the question. However, he was compelled, by fresh instances, to make a new appeal to the kindness of the Pope. He hinted at the matter in an audience, and saw, as he informs us, by Leo's quietly mischievous look, that he was not to be taken by surprise. Varying his hexameter, but coming to the same conclusion, he replied,

Sunt mores, doctrina, genus; sed deficit aetas.[3]

He added, that he had an ample record in his mind of the merit, virues qualities, and claims of the Abbé de Rohan, arranged in good verses, but every one of them ended by the same dactyl and spondee.

It was well known, however, that he would have willingly have introduced into the Sacred College the venerable bishop of Hermopolis, Monseigneur Frayssinous, had not his modesty absolutely resisted every effort of the Pope[4] to obtain his acceptance.

1. [King I cannot be; prince I do not wish to be; I am a Rohan.]
2. [His spirit, piety and virtues are there, but he lacks maturity.]
3. [His morals, doctrine and breeding are there, but he lacks maturity.]
4. Chevalier D'Artaud, *Vie de Pius VIII.*

It was not till 1830, that de Rohan, being now Archbishop of Besançon, was promoted by Pius VIII. In the
revolution which shortly followed in France, he was inter-
cepted by the mob, and treated with great indignity; a
circumstance which probably greatly shortened his life. For
he died in February 1833, in his 42nd year.

Very different is the cardinalate bestowed on our coun-
tryman Thomas Weld. It has been seen that the hat which
Leo XII wished to bestow on Bishop Baines, in gratitude to
the Benedictine Order, was given by Pius VIII to F. Frascini,
at the very beginning of his Pontificate, to be enjoyed for
only a very brief space. Cardinal Weld was named partly in
consideration of his own personal claims, partly also to second a desire of seeing an Englishman among the highest
dignitaries of the Church. Why, it was asked—and the Pope
could not fail to see the justice of the question—should
almost every nation be represented in that body to which is
entrusted the management of religious affairs throughout
the world, except the one whose language is spoken by a
great proportion of its Christian inhabitants? Not only the
British Islands, but the United States, the East and West
Indies, Canada, the Cape, Australia, and the islands of the
Pacific, were in daily communication with the Holy See,
and with the Congregation of Propaganda, which attended
to their wants. Was it not reasonable, that near the ruling
Chair, and in the number of its counsellors, there should be
at least one who might represent the immense race,
endowed with its intelligence, familiar with its wants and
its forms of expressing them, as well as with the peculiar
position in which many portions were placed? It would
seem hardly fair to deny this, or to murmur at its being
acted on.

The person first selected for this honourable post, was one
who certainly could never have looked forward to it as his
future lot. He was born in London, January 22, 1773, and
was the oldest son of Thomas Weld of Lulworth Castle, and
Mary Stanley, who belonged to the elder and Catholic

branch of the Stanley family, now extinct. He was educated entirely at home; and early gave proof of his great piety and munificent charity. This was particularly displayed in favour of the many religious communities which the French revolution threw like shipwrecked families on our coast. He treated them with utmost kindness, received them into his very house, and provided for all their wants. This he first did concurrently with his excellent father; but he continued all his good works after his parent's death, or rather increased them. The Trappist nuns were received at Lulworth; and. with rare generosity, Mr Weld bought from them, when they quitted his estate, the buildings, to him worthless, which they had been allowed, and even assisted to raise. The poor Clares from Gravelines, and the nuns of the Visitation, who took refuge, the first at Plymouth, and the second at Shepton Mallet, were special objects of his bounty.

In the mean time he had married, and had been blessed with a daughter, the worthy representative of the hereditary virtues of his house. He had taken, and worthily filled, his place in society; he had done the honours of his house with liberality and dignity, had pursued the the duties of the English gentleman in his noblest character, acted as a country magistrate, enjoyed country sports, and reciprocated hospitality with his neighbours. It is well known that George III in his sojourns at Weymouth used to visit Lulworth, and always expressed the greatest regard for the Cardinal's family. What life could have been less considered the way to ecclesiastical honours than this of a Dorsetshire country squire, in the field, or at his board?

Yet they who knew him intimately, and had watched through his life the virtue that distingushed and the piety which sanctified it, were not surprised to find him, after the death of his excellent consort in 1815, and the marriage of his daughter in 1818 to the eldest son of that sterling nobleman Lord Clifford, abandoning the world, resigning his estates to his next brother, their present worthy occupier, of yachting celebrity, and removing on an annual pension to Paris to embrace the ecclesiastical state. He was ordained priest in 1821, by the Archbishop of that city.

He returned to England, and entered on the usual duties of the priesthood at Chelsea, and continued his liberal exercise of charity till the Bishop Vicar-Apostolic of Upper Canada, obtained his appointment as his coadjutor. He received, accordingly, the episcopal consecration on the 6th of August, 1826. He remained in England, partly for the transaction of business, partly for reasons of health. During the space of three years, while he *tacitis regnabat Amyclis*—for he was bishop *in partibus* of that classical city[1]—he lived at Hammersmith, directing there a community of Benedictine nuns.

He was then invited to Rome for higher purposes, at the same time that his daughter's health required change of climate, and it was natural for him to accompany her. On the 25th of May, 1830, he was named Cardinal by Pius VIII.

Such a new and unexpected occurrence might have been variously interpreted, according to party views; and it would have been naturally expected, that expression would be given to these conflicting feelings. This, at any rate, was not the case in Rome. Unanimous and unequivocal was the expression of opinion among English residents and travellers there. All flocked to the reception given by the new Cardinal, and manifested their satisfaction at such a manifestation of good-will towards his country. And similar were the expressions of feeling that reached him from home. In the funeral oration[2] delivered at his sumptious obsequies performed by order of his son-in-law, Lord Clifford, on the 22nd of April, 1837, is the following sentence: "He received assurances from persons of high influence and dignity, that his nomination had excited no jealousy, as of old, but on the contrary, had afforded satisfaction to those

1. Not the Italian one, however, to which the verse and epithet refers.
2. Printed in English and Italian in Rome in that year.

whom every Englishman esteems and reveres: individuals,
who at home are known to indulge in expression of decided
hostility to Rome, and to our holy religion, recognised in
him a representative of both, whom they venerated and
gladly approached; and when his hospitable mansion was
thrown open to his countrymen, I believe that never was
the sternest professor of a different creed known to decline
the honour, which the invitation of the English Cardinal
was acknowledged to confer."

The first part only of this sentence can require any explanation. It shows the circumstance alluded to was
sufficiently public to have passed the bounds of delicate
reserve. Indeed, it is too honourable to all parties to need
being shrouded under any secrecy. Soon after his elevation,
Cardinal Weld received a letter from the natural guardian
to the heiress to the Throne, introducing a distinguished
member of her household, in which he was assured not only
that his promotion had given satisfaction to the exalted circle to which she belonged, but that should he ever visit
England, he would be received by that family with the
repect which was his due. Such is the impressed recollection of this interesting and generously-minded document,
read at the time.

Of course, a few years later, its practical ratification would
have had to depend upon the possible humour of a minister,
rather than on any nobler impulses of a royal mind. But
there can be no doubt that on this occasion there was no
jealousy or anger felt anywhere: perhaps the known virtues
and retired life of the new Cardinal gained him this universal benevolence; perhaps the press saw nothing to gain by
agitating the nation on the subject. Certain it is, however,
that the promotion was made by the free choice of the Pontiff, without any presentation from England, or any
consultation with its government. In this respect, it stands
in marked contrast with that of even a De Rohan.

It could not be expected that, at the mature age which
Cardinal Weld had reached, he would be master in a new

language, or perfectly learn the ways of transacting high ecclesiastical business; nor had the occupations of his life, nor even his brief studies, been calculated to make equal to those who from youth had been devoted to legal and theological pursuits. The Cardinal most wisely provided for these necessary deficiencies. For his theological adviser he selected Professor Fornari, one of the most eminent divines in Rome, who was soon after sent as Nuncio first to Belgium and then to Paris; and was himself elevated in due time to the dignity on which his counsels had shed such lustre. For secretaries, at different times, he had the present Bishop of Plymouth, Dr Vaughan, and the Abbate De Luca, afterwards made Bishop of Aversa, and actually Nuncio at Vienna; a man of more than ordinary learning and ability, well-versed, even before, in English literature, as well as in that of his own and other countries.

As his share, the Cardinal brought into his council sterling good sense and sincere humility; and soon acquired considerable influence in the congregations or departments of ecclesiastical affairs to which he was attached. At the same time he was genuinely courteous, hospitable. and obliging. His apartments in the Odescalchi Palace were spendidly furnished, and periodically filled with the aristocracy of Rome, native and foreign, and with multitudes of his countrymen, all of whom found him always willing to render them any service. Indeed, if he had a fault, it was the excessiveness of his kindness, too often undiscriminating in its objects, and liable to be imposed upon by the designing or the unworthy. But surely, if one must look back, at life's close, upon some past frailty, it would not be this defect that would beget most remorse.

That end soon came. The life of close application and seclusion, in a southern climate, taken up at an age when the constitution is no longer pliant, could not be engrafted easily on a youth of vigorous activity spent among the breezy moors of the Dorsetshire hills. Great sensibility to cold and atmospheric change gradually became perceptible, and at length assumed the form of a pulmonary disease. Surrounded by his family, and strengthened by every religious succour, the Cardinal sank calmly into the repose of the just, on the 10th of April, 1837. Seldom has a stranger been more deeply and feelingly regretted by the inhabitants of a city, than was this holy man by the poor of Rome.

CHAPTER IV

THE PRINCIPAL EVENTS OF THE THE PONTIFICATE

IF the the short duration of Pius the Eighth's reign has been pleaded in excuse for paucity of events and of recollections, it cannot be adduced as a reason for the want of great and even startling occurrences. For in the course of a few months may be concentrated many such, full of portentous consequences; and in them were probably deposited the *semina rerum*, which a future generation will not suffice to unfold into perfect growth. Such a period was the narrow space comprised in this pontificate. Three or four signal occurrences will suffice to verify this assertion.

And first—to begin with the very outset of Pius' pontificate—he was elected March 31, 1829; and, scarcely a month later, it was my pleasing duty to communicate to him the gladsome tidings of Catholic Emancipation. This great and just measure received the royal assent on the 23rd of April following.

It need hardly be remarked, that such a message was one of unbounded joy, and might well have been communicated to the Head of the Catholic Church in the words by which the arrival of paschal time is announced to him every year: *"Pater Sancte, annuntio vobis gaudium magnum."* To him, who was not only most intelligent, but alive to all that passed throughout Christendom, the full meaning of this measure was of course apparent. But generally it was not so.

In foreign countries, the conditions of Catholics in Great Britain was but little understood. The religion, not the political state, of their fellow-believers mainly interested other nations. Through all the continent, Catholicity in this empire was supposed to be confined to Ireland; and, again and again an English Catholic traveller has heard himself corrected when he has so described himself, by such an expression as this: "Of course you mean Irish?" In fact, even as late as the period we are dwelling on, when languages were as yet not much studied, and there was a more feeble circulation of periodical literature, less travel too, and slender international relations, the mutual ignorance of countries was very great. Nor, either then or now, could one venture to say that there was or is more true acquaintance with other nations among the population of England, than there is accurate knowledge of our island in Continental states.

The constitution of this country, especially complicated as it is to ourselves, was a puzzle to races accustomed to a simple monarchy for ages, and scarcely possessing experience of anything between that and bare republicanism. To tell them that Catholics in Great Britain were excluded from seats in Parliament, bore perhaps with many no more sense of hardship than to hear that they were not allowed a place in the Turkish Divan. They could not appreciate the influence and importance of the position, nor the insufferable insult of a perpetual and hereditary incapacity for it. Hence our public rejoicing at the acquisition of this coveted boon was unintelligible to the multitude.

After an audience of the Pope, the Vice Rector of the College, now Archbishop of Trebizond) and myself visited the Secretary of State, and received from him warm expressions of congratulation. We then proceeded to make preparations for our festival, on the usual Roman plan. The front of our house was covered with an elegant architectural design in variegated lamps, and an orchestra was erected opposite for festal music. In the morning of the appointed

day, a Te Deum, attended by the various British colleges
was performed; in the afternoon a banquet on a munificent
scale was given at his villa near St Paul's, by Monsignor
Nicolai, the learned illustrator of that Basilica; and in the
evening we returned home to see the upturned faces of multitudes reflecting the brilliant "lamps of architecture" that
tapestried our venerable walls. But the words "*Emanci-
pazione Cattolica,*" which were emblazoned in lamps along
the front, were read by people with difficulty, and interpreted by conjecture; so that many came and admired, but went
away, unenlightened by the blaze that dazzled them, into
the darkness visible of surrounding streets.

In fact the first of the two words, long and formidable to
untutored lips, was no household word in Italy; nor was
there any imaginable connection in ordinary persons'
minds between it and its adjective, nor between the two
and England. But to us and our guests there was surely a
magic in the words, that spoke to our hearts, and awakened
there sweet music, more cheering than that of our orchestra, and kindled up a brighter illumination in our minds
than upon the walls. We had left our country when young,
and hardly conscious of the wrongs which galled our
elders; we should return to it in possession of our rights;
and thus have hardly experienced more sense of injury
than they who have been born since that happy era. So
some of us could feel; and had not this its uses? Whatever
may be considered the disadvantages of a foreign education, it possessed, especially at that period, this very great
advantage, that it reared the mind, and nursed the affections, beyond the reach of religious contests and their
irritation. No "winged words" of anger or scorn, however
powerfully fledged for flight, could well surmount the Alps;
and if they did, the venom must have dropped from their
tip, as this must have lost its pungency, in so long a course.
Scarcely any amount of roaring on platforms could have
sent even a softened whisper across the sea; and the con-
tinuous attacks of a hostile press could only reach one in

the broken fragments that occasionally tesselated a foreign paper. Thus, one hardly knew of the bitter things said against what was dearest to us; and certainly I will bear willing testimony to the absence of all harsh words and uncharitable insinuations against others in public lectures and private teaching, or even in conversation, at Rome.

One grows up there in a kinder spirit, and learns to speak of error in gentler tone, than elsewhere, though in the very centre of highest orthodox feeling. Still, if wrongs had not been keenly felt, the act of justice so honourable to one's country, and the sense of relief from degrading trammels, made every British Catholic heart rejoice in Rome, when the news reached us, that the struggle of years had been crowned with triumph, and that the laurels of a peaceful Waterloo had graced the same brows as were crowned by the wreaths of our last great sanguinary victory.[1]

This is certainly not the place to descant upon this subject; but it was too mighty a political act to have quietly subsided in a moment among the other enactments of a session, or to be quoted as only one chapter of the statutes passed in a given year. The generation still exists which had led life and action before the momentous step. Many survive it who regret even bitterly the good old days of exclusion, which amounted to monopoly for them and theirs: some too remain whose shackles were removed, but not the numbness and cramp which they had produced. By degrees society will consist more and more, and then entirely, of those who have grown up side by side from infancy under the fostering of impartial laws, in the feeling of essential equality, without consciousness or pretension of this having been a concession.

The remembrance of a condition of things, when one portion of the same community was a suppliant to the other

1. The reference is to the Duke of Wellington who led the Administration which successfuly piloted the Catholic Emancipation Act through Parliament in 1829, as well as earlier commanding the British forces at the battle of Waterloo in 1815, which finally ended the Napoleonic Wars.

for common rights, will have passed away; and with it the pride of having refused or of having granted, and the humiliation of having long been spurned, and at last almost compulsorily relieved. Then, and only then, will that clear stage have been prepared, on which peaceful and intellectual contention can be conducted as between champions in ancient times; devoid of hate and of heat, and uninfluenced by recollections of mutual relations, then unknown to either side. But, certainly, the day that prepared such a prospect for a country divided in religion, may well be considered a bright one in the brief annals of the pontificate within which it fell.

The second striking occurrence of Pius's pontificate should rather bear another name; it is a measure more than an event, proceeding from the Pope himself, of immense moment at the time, but not destined to produce its startling effects till seven years after his death. At a time when the anxieties, pains, and contention which this measure caused have been soothed and almost forgotten, at a moment when all are rejoicing at the coming alliance between the power to which it related and our own royal family, it would be ill-timed and ungracious to enter any details of the Pope's celebrated answer to four great German prelates on the subject of mixed marriages.

They had consulted his predecessor on the conduct to be observed respecting them, not on general principles, but in connection with civil legislation, at variance with ecclesiastical law; whereby their consciences were sorely perplexed. It was for them some such position as clergymen of the Established Church declared themselves to hold last year, in consequence of the new Divorce Act. They both considered the law of the land to conflict with that of God; but in the one case each person had to consult his own conscience alone, or many might contribute their individual convictions to a common fund of remonstrance, or a joint engine of resistance; in the other all had recourse to a recognised superior in spirituals, and head in Church government, who could speak as one having authority, and whom they would all obey.

Pius, as Cardinal Castiglioni, had gone fully into the case, and was, therefore, prepared for action. Before the close of the first year of his reign, he addressed his notable Brief to the Archbishop of Cologne, and the Bishops of Treves, Paderborn, and Münster, which was immediately followed by a long practical instruction bearing the signature of Cardinal Albani.

There is no intention of discussing the grounds or motives of this document; nor of going into the nature of its provisions; still less of justifying the Pope's conduct. Our purpose only requires of us the more pleasing task, that of characterising the paper itself. Reading it now, after seventeen years, one cannot fail to be struck by the calm and apostolic dignity which pervades it in every part. It is known that it cost the gentle, yet firm, mind of Pius a conflict of emotions, which inflicted on him almost anguish. His office compelled him to reply: and the answer could not be any but a censure of a powerful state, with which he was perfectly at peace; and directions to thwart its measure, and testify to the utmost "abhorrence" for it. It was impossible for him to foresee the possible results of his decided conduct. His directions might be disobeyed, and the world might deride his innocuous blow, as though, like the feeble old Priam's,

— "*telum imbelle sine ictu.*"[1]

they might be carried out not in his spirit, and confusion and misunderstanding would arise. Or even they might be admirably obeyed, and yet lead to confusion and conflicts, to sufferings and violence, of which the blame would probably be cast on himself. It was painful therefore, in the extreme, to feel obliged to issue such a document; but, upon its face no sign can be traced of the agitation and affliction of his soul. It is impassive and dignified throughout. There are blended in it two qualities not often combined: its

1. [His unwarlike spear that had never struck a blow.] (Virgil; *The Aeneid*: Bk II, 544).

enactments are as clear and as definite as any statute could make them, without wavering, flinching or aught extenuating; at the same time, its entire tone is conciliatory, respectful, and even friendly. To the bishops he speaks as a father and a master: of their sovereign he undeviatingly writes as of a fellow monarch, an ally, and a friend. His confidence in the royal justice, fairness and tolerance, is entire and unbounded. The character of Pius is breathed into every paragraph, his inflexibility of conscience, his strictness of principle, with its kindness of heart, and gentleness of natural disposition. Moreover, the consummate canonist is discoverable to the more learned, and this too in the line of condescension and conciliation. His successor, in 1837, commenting on this Brief, justly remarked that it "pushed its indulgence so far, that one might truly say it reached the very boundary line which could not be passed without violation of duty." Every one knows what a nicety in legal knowledge this requires. A well-remembered popular leader used to boast, that he trusted so confidently in his accurate acquaintance with law, that he had no fear of overstepping its limits, or being caught in the snares which he knew beset his path. His foot was, however, at length entangled in their meshes; his confidence had betrayed him, and his energy was irreparably broken.

Not so was it with Pius. What he had written, he had written, in the fulness of a wisdom which holiness of life had matured, and an earnest sense of duty now doubly enlightened; not a word of it had to be recalled, modified, or compromised.; and, though after a long struggle, it has remained an oracle and a law. But, as has been remarked, he only committed a seed to the furrow, and he lived not to pluck its bearing. For more than a year this document lay buried in some ministerial bureau at Berlin: it was then taken up, negotiated about, and cast for three more years into oblivion. What followed belongs to another Pontificate; but will not even there need fresh attention. Suffice it to say, that the scars of old wounds are healed; the Roman purple glows upon the archiepiscopal throne of glorious Cologne, almost rebuilt under royal patronage; the young Prince, future heir to the Prussian crown, who is about to take into partnership of its brilliancy and its burthen England's first daughter, has known, and been known by, Rome with reciprocated esteem; while the monarch who will welcome them home has, on many occasions, given proof of his own personal feelings in favour of justice and fair dealing towards the newer, as well as the older, provinces of his kingdom.

Two important public events thus marked the commencement and middle of this brief pontificate: the first was joyful, the second painful; a third and still more disastrous one preceded, and perhaps prepared, its close. Like others, it only developed its consequences in another pontificate.

In July, 1830, took place the first of those great political earthquakes which have since become so frequent; shaking down thrones, and scattering their occupants, without war, and comparatively without the cruelties of a violent reaction. Three days formed the mystic term required for the overthrow of a dynasty: street-barricading and domiciliary slaughter were the strategy employed; then all was over, without guillotine or fusillades. Such were the three days, once called glorious in France, commemorated by anniversary festivities. The elder branch of the Bourbons was its victim; the work of many years' war by confederated Europe, was overthrown in a trice; down to its favourite and tenderest shoot, it was whirled entire, by the revolutionary blast, across the sea to a second exile, but scarcely to a second hospitable welcome. And yet the fight and the turmoil, the agitation and the waste of strength, did not bring about a change of name. When the dust and smoke had cleared away, another Bourbon was on the throne; a monarch had succeeded to a monarch; a younger branch more vigorous in its offshoots, fuller of younger sap, was planted on the same spot, or rather sprang from the same trunk as the one so mercilessly lopped. It appeared as if France had not at least quarreled with its root.

In August, the terrible lesson, easily learnt, was faithfully repeated in Brussels, and Belgium was forever separated from Holland. To those who had witnessed the first great revolution in France, the reappearance once more, in the same country, of the quelled spirit of that event could not but be a spectacle full of terrors. The recollection of that sanguinary period was still fresh in the memory of many. Charles X, who was expelled by the new revolution, was, after all, the brother of the king who had perished on the scaffold in the first; this alone brought the two events into close connection.

Pius VIII had lived and suffered in one; he could not but be deeply affected by another. It was easy to foresee that examples so successful as these must encourage the discontented of other countries, and that a spark from one conflagration might suffice to set drier materials of other dynasties in a blaze. His own dominions were not left in peace. The storm which was soon to break in all its fury, was gathering slowly and sullenly around. Soon after his accession, he renewed the edicts of his predecessor against secret societies—the Carbonari. A lodge of these conspirators was discovered in Rome, and twenty-six of its members were arrested. A special commission was appointed to try them; one was condemned to death, some others sentenced to imprisonment. The first was grand-master and chief of the conspiracy. But Pius commuted his sentence, and mercifully spared his life.

These repeated shocks abroad and at home, to which may be added the revolution in Poland in November, and the death of his friend and ally the King of Naples, inflicted stroke after stroke on the Pope's shattered frame. The malignant humour which had affected him so long outwardly, was driven inwards upon more vital organs, and threatened, towards the end of 1830, a speedy dissolution.

In the meantime, Pius had taken a plain, straightforward course. No sooner had the French revolution proved complete, and Louis-Philippe had been seated firmly on his throne, than he frankly recognised his government, and confirmed the credentials of his own Nuncio. The Archbishop of Paris, Monseigneur De Quélen, a man whose virtues all must admire, demurred to this decision, and sent an envoy to Rome, to argue the question of the new oath of fidelity, and of public prayers for the head of State. Several other bishops likewise entertained similar conscientious scruples, and consulted the same supreme authority. On the 29th of September, the Pope addressed a most luminous and kind brief to the Archbishop, in which he replied to his doubts, and assured him that he might safely accord both the required pledges of fidelity.

It cannot be necessary to remark, how fearfully the outbreak of revolutionary spirit which made its first appearance in this pontificate, was pregnant with immense results throughout the Continent; how it was only the first of successive convulsions in France; visited successively greater and lesser states, from empires to grand-duchies; and has led to more changes of dynasties, more resignations of sovereigns, more variations of national constitutions, more provisional governments, more periods of anarchy, more civil strife, more military rule, more states of siege, more political assassinations, more disturbance of international law, and more subversion of the moral bases of society,— crowded and condensed in one quarter of a century,— than would run diluted through the annals of an hundred years in the world's history.

The good Pope was spared the sight of all this misery. For, as the reader has seen, the beginning of this revolutionary movement seemed to cut short his valuable life. He was conscious of his approaching end, and asked to receive the Sacraments, which the highest and lowest in the church equally require and desire; or rather which bind us all together in an equality of helplessness and of relief;—like the food of the body in this, that the monarch and the beggar must both partake of it; unlike it in this, that only one quality and one measure is served out to both. A Pope ordains like an ordinary bishop, recites his breviary like a common priest, receives the Viaticum under one species, the same as any patient in the hospital, and goes through the humble duty of confession, generally to a simple priest, like the everyday sinner of the world. In what is believed to be supernatural, and belongs to the order of grace, he is on a level with his own children. He can give more than they, but he must receive the same.

But a trait is recorded of the dying Pius, which will justify, or illustrate, what has been said concerning the delicacy of his conscience as well as the disinterestedness of his conduct. On his death-bed, he sent for his treasurer, Cristaldi, and requested him, in virtue of the powers vested in his office, to secure a small pension for life to one old and faithful domestic, who had attended him for years. He had laid by nothing himself, from which he could provide for him; and he doubted whether he had himself a right to leave the treasury burthened with this trifling personal gratuity. He expressed his thankfulness when his request was efficiently complied with, and composed himself to rest.[1]

One the morning of December the first, Pius VIII, calmly breathed his last.

In the recollections of the preceding Popes, the reader will have observed one principle kept in view, which he may think has been lost sight of in the record of this pontificate. It has been wished to exemplify, even at the risk of being personal—which recollections must necessarily be— how individual is the influence of the Holy See upon all, however insignificant, who closely approach it. The shade of a tall and stately tree, if it be of baneful character, blights all that is planted beneath it; while another seems to draw upwards, and to give straight, though perhaps slender growth to what springs up under its shelter. Such is the benign and fostering protection and direction which many

1. Chevalier D'Artaud.

will have experienced in the Roman Pontiff. And, therefore, a recollection of having been brought beneath this propitious influence is equivalent to a consciousness of having felt it. Already one conversation with Pius VIII has been recorded, which turned on those studies which formed the writer's favourite pursuits, and was calculated to encourage perseverance in them. Another interview can more easily be here inserted, because it has already been published many years, and, therefore, is as much the reader's property as the author's own. The following is an extract from the last of twelve lectures, delivered in Rome in 1835, and published in London in the following year:—

"In my own case, I should be unjust to overlook this opportunity of saying that, on every occasion, but principally on the subject of these Lectures,[1] I have received condescending encouragement from those whose approbation every Catholic will consider his best reward."

"To this acknowledgment was appended the following explanatory note:—

"I feel a pleasure in relating the following anecdote. A few years ago, I prefixed a thesis held by a member of the English College (afterwards the Right Reverend Bishop Baggs), a Latin dissertation of ten or twelve pages, upon the necessity of uniting general and scientific knowledge to theological pursuits. I took a rapid view of different branches of learning discussed in these Lectures. The essay was soon translated into Italian, and printed in a Sicilian journal; and, I believe, appeared also in Milan. What was most gratifying, however, to my own feelings, and may serve as a confirmation of the assertions in the text, is, that when, two days after, I waited upon the late Pius VIII, a man truly versed in sacred and profane literature, to present him, according to usage, with a copy of the thesis prepared for him, I found him with it on his table; and, in the kindest terms, he informed me, that, having heard of my little

1. "Lectures on the Connection between Science and Revealed Religion."

Essay, he had instantly sent for it, and added, in terms allusive to the figure quoted above from the ancient Fathers: 'You have robbed Egypt of its spoil, and shown that it belongs to the people of God.' "

This was the watering, soft and genial, of that little germ, which made it grow up, at least with the vigour of good intentions, into something more complete. These few condescending words gave new zest to researches commenced, imparted value to what had already been gathered, and encouragement towards collecting what still lay scattered. They shed a cheerful brightness over one period of life. And that very moment might not be unjustly considered its very midpoint. We all look back, from our lengthening desert path, upon some such green and sunlit oasis from which we started; but what was more, mine was then peopled and alive with kindred minds. It is then, that, on reaching back through memory to that happier time, to me

> *Occurrunt animae, quales neque candidiores*
> *Terra tulit, neque queis me sit devinctior alter.*[1].

During that brief and long-passed era of life, congenial pursuits created links of which few now remain, between the survivor and many well more worthy to have lived. Not to speak of Italy, and many great and good men who flourished there, especially in Rome, it is pleasant to remember having conversed, and sometime corresponded, with such scholars in France as the patriarch of Oriental literature, Sylvestre de Sacy;[2] the rival of Grotefend[3] and precursor

1. Horace, *Sermones* Bk.1.5, 51-2. [Souls present themselves—and neither has earth produced such resplendent ones as these, nor would another prove more devoted to them than I.]

2. De Sacy, Silvestre (1758-1838), orientalist and Professor of Persian at the Collège de France.

3. Grotefend, Georg Friederich (1775-1853), philologist who deciphered the cuneiform inscriptions at Persepolis.

of Rawlinson,[1] Saint-Martin;[2] the inaugurator, almost, of
Tartar and Mongolian learning, Abel-Rémusat;[3] not to
mention Balbi,[4] Ozanam,[5] Halma,[6] and many others: and
in Germany to have been in similar relations with
Möhler,[7] Klee,[8]—both too early taken from us,—Scholz,[9]
Schlegel,[10] Windischmann[11] the elder, and the two
noble-minded Görreses,[12] the philospher of the noblest
faculties, and the poet of the sweetest affections.

Many others, indeed, as yet survive, to share the recollections of that period, which we hold together as a
mutual bond of friendly intercourse and undeviating sympathies: but we all of us must now and then cast a
"longing, lingering look behind," and turn away with a
sigh, to see our old oasis still green and sunny, but principally with that sheen which faith reflects upon the graves
of the holy and the wise.

1. Rawlinson, Sir Henry (1810-1895), British assyriologist, who deciphered the Persian cuneiform inscriptions at Behistan.

2. Saint Martin, leading French linguistic scholar.

3. Rémusat, Jean-Pierre Abel (1788-1832), specialist in Chinese and
Tartar linguistics.

4. Balbi, Adriano (1784-1848), geographer and statistician; author of
Ethnographique du Globe (1824) and Abrégé de Géographie (1832).

5. Ozanam, Fréderic (1813-53) scholar and literary critic.

6. Halm, Karl Felix (1809-1882), classical philologist who worked especially on Cicero and Quintillian.

7. Möhler, Johann Adam (1796-1838), theologian and professor at
Munich whose writings carefully analyse the differences between
Catholicism and Protestantism.

8. Klee, Heinrich (1800-40), theologian, succeeded Möhler at Munich.

9. Scholz, Johann (1794-1853), priest & professor of theology at Bonn.

10. Von Schlegel, Friederich (1772-1829), celebrated German critic and
philologist; younger brother of August Wilhelm von Schlegel; both were
converts to Catholicism and had a profound influence on the Romantic
movement.

11. Von Windischmann, Karl Josef (1775-1839, German philosopher of
history.

12. Von Görreses; Josef (1776-1848) was professor of history at Munich whose
work suggests how many nations' myths reflect monotheistic revelation.

Most recent books

PIUS THE SEVENTH

Cardinal Wiseman knew Pius VII from his boyhoood days at the Venerable English College in Rome. This is his fascinating account of Pius's life and times covering his brutal expulsion from Rome and imprisonment by Napoleon and his eventual triumphant restoration as ruler of the Papal States. A companion to Wisemen's account of Leo XII and Pius VIII in this volume.

148 pages   £8.99

THE CARDINAL'S SNUFF-BOX

A villa in the Italian lake district, in a summer of the late 1890s; a castle in a garden, a lake, and snow-capped mountains in the distance; a beautiful woman glimpsed a few times in the past; a young aspiring novelist.

In this elegant novel Henry Harland has combined an amusing and observant narrative with an exploration of opposing religious and philosophical views of life, which are ultimately reconciled by a pig, a storm, and a cardinal with the help of his snuff-box.

170 pages   £8.99

SET THE ECHOES FLYING
AN ANTHOLOGY OF POEMS, SONGS AND HYMNS

This includes most of the favourites of England, Ireland, Scotland, and Wales. Five hundred years of pieces to inspire, amuse and comfort. A bedside book for all ages, and acknowledged the best of its kind since General Wavell's *Other Men's Flowers* published in the 1940s.

272 pages   *with illustrations by Mary Tyler*   £10.99

Other titles

Pilgrims to Jerusalem: accounts of visits to the Holy Land	£12.99
Robert Hugh Benson: Confessions of a Convert	£5.99
Elizabeth Butler—Battle Painter: Autobiography	£7.99
G K Chesterton: Autobiography (2nd edition)	£11.99
G.K. Chesterton: A Short History of England	£9.99
William Cobbett: A History of the Protestant Reformation	£9.99
F Marion Crawford: The Heart of Rome (novel)	£7.99
Hugh Dormer DSO : War Diary	£7.99
Bernard Holland: Memoir of Kenelm Digby	£6.99
Helen Jackson: Ramona (novel)	£8.99
Antony Matthew: Pearl of Great Price	£5.95
John Henry Newman: Collected Poems & Dream of Gerontius	£8.99
Coventry Patmore: The Bow set in the Cloud (his best critical writings)	£8.99
Francis Thompson: Collected Poems	£9.99

If you have difficulty in purchasing Fisher Press titles from bookshops you may acquire them direct from Fisher Press, Post Office Box 42, Sevenoaks, Kent, England. Telephone/Fax: 01732 761830.